Search for the Soul in Everyday Living

THE MOTHER
compiled by
Wayne Bloomquist

PUBLISHER:
LOTUS LIGHT PUBLICATIONS
P.O. Box 2
Wilmot, WI 53192 U.S.A.

FIRST U.S. EDITION Nov. 24, 1990

Published by Lotus Light Publications
by arrangement with Wayne Bloomquist
and Sri Aurobindo Ashram Trust.

ISBN: 0-941524-57-4

Library of Congress Catalog Card Number 89-85343

Printed in the United States of America

CONTENTS:

SRI AUROBINDO
(1872–1950)

Born in Calcutta. Educated in England from the age of seven. Returned to India in 1893. After 13 years of service—mainly teaching—in Baroda State, he moved to Calcutta where he devoted himself to India's struggle for independence. In 1910 he went to Pondicherry to pursue exclusively his spiritual quest. His works have been published in the 30 volumes of Sri Aurobindo Birth Centenary Library collection.

THE MOTHER
(1878–1973)

Born in Paris as Mirra Alfassa. Studied art, music and occultism. Met Sri Aurobindo in 1914 in Pondicherry and went to live there in 1920. Became Sri Aurobindo's collaborator and was given full charge of Sri Aurobindo Ashram (founded in 1926) where she came to be called the Mother. Her teachings have been published in the Collected Works of the Mother, which to date comprise 16 volumes.

From: *Living Within, A. S. Dalal, Institute of Integral Psychology, Ojai, California, 1987.*

INTRODUCTION

This Anthology of the Mother's Writings has evolved from my original intent to collect some exercises on the expansion of our consciousness.

It is amazing the number of gems we often have on our own bookshelves just waiting to be discovered. Over the past twenty years I have read many segments of the Question and Answer series, which comprise seven volumes recorded during the period 1950 to 1958 and one volume in 1929 from talks to students, teachers and ashramites on a variety of topics. But it was only in 1986 that I began to read them all systematically when I kept seeing passage after passage that I had to note, mainly, about various exercises, i.e., something that one could practice either alone or as part of a group. Participants in a study group could take an exercise and each would practice in his/her own way and then share this experience at the next meeting. It would be a way of not only promoting self-growth but also getting to know other participants. I have been in too many groups where there was either no or all personal interaction. This interaction may not be necessary in an Ashram where there are numerous support systems, many are very subtle, but it is much more difficult in our society to have any sustained continuity in higher consciousness.

After I had assembled all of the selected pages and had reorganized them, I discovered my project had evolved to its present state (this is the first volume) as a primer in Integral Yoga. It is my hope that one can get a sense of the purpose of Sri Aurobindo and the Mother through her conversations. The Mother has few peers in expressing succinctly in simple English (translated from the French) the most profound truths.

We are now going through a very troubled period. The intensity in the atmosphere is creating inconceivable, bizarre behavior but, parenthetically, the opportunity for truly tremendous self growth. Very possibly this is a period that has never been experienced on the planet. At this time it is difficult to see beyond the chaos and the despair; however, it is not unexpected. Sri Aurobindo was writing about the transformation occurring now as early as 1910. It has been a long time coming and I am grateful for the privilege to be able to participate. I hope this volume will broaden your perspective and kindle your aspiration in the glorious struggle ahead.

Wayne E. Bloomquist
Berkeley, California

All the world's possibilities in man
Are waiting as the tree waits in its seed:
His past lives in him; it drives his future's pace;
His present's acts fashion his coming fate.
The unborn gods hide in his house of Life.

Savitri

1

TO BE CONSCIOUS

Our ordinary perception of consciousness is that we are either conscious, when we are awake, or unconscious, when we are asleep. This chapter "To Be Conscious" will quickly dispel that notion when we begin to ask ourselves such questions as: What is our purpose in living? Is our Physical World our only reality? Who Am I?

Along with our beginning to learn about this multi-dimensional universe we live in and this multi-dimensional being we call ourselves, other questions can arise about such things as difficulties, changing our habits, cleansing our subconscious mind and the interplay of forces.

One of the implications of "becoming conscious" is to know the Divine Will. In order to reach this state, we, as individuals, must have a unified will. We must also have a degree of coherence of the numerous aspects of our own being so that we can ultimately expand from our isolated egocentric consciousness to the Vast, the Wideness of Being.

Finally, when we become more conscious of other realities and other states of being and consciousness, and we have a concern and a love for this planet, we need to find a way to integrate these apparent opposites, Spirit and Matter. This has a practical application as to how we infuse these inner realizations into our work and into our personal life to create an integrated being.

What Is Our Purpose in Living?*

And one day, you ask yourself, "But then, why is one

*these headings are the editor's.

born? Why does one die? Why does one suffer? Why does one act?"

You no longer live like a little machine, hardly half-conscious. You want to feel truly, to act truly, to know truly. Then, in ordinary life one searches for books, for people who know a little more than oneself, one begins to seek somebody who can solve these questions, lift the veil of ignorance. Here it is very simple. You only have to . . . do the things one does every day, but to do them with a purpose.

You go to the Samadhi,[1] look at Sri Aurobindo's picture, you come to receive a flower from me, sit down to a lesson; you do everything you do but . . . with one question within you: Why?

And then, if you ask the question, you receive the answer.

Why?

Because we don't want life as it is any longer, because we don't want falsehood and ignorance any longer, because we don't want suffering and unconsciousness any longer, because we do not want disorder and bad will any longer, because Sri Aurobindo has come to tell us: It is not necessary to leave the earth to find the Truth, it is not necessary to leave life to find one's soul, it is not necessary to give up the world or to have limited beliefs in order to enter into relation with the Divine. The Divine is everywhere, in everything, and if He is hidden . . . it is because we do not take the trouble to discover Him.

We can, simply by a sincere aspiration, open a sealed door in us and find . . . that Something which will change the whole significance of life, reply to all our questions, solve all our problems and lead us to the perfection we aspire for without knowing it, to that Reality which *alone* can satisfy and give us lasting joy, equilibrium, strength, life. (9-374,375)

Our Physical World Is Only One Reality

The material is a plane, isn't it?

Yes, it is a final result. There is an increasing materiality and a decreasing materiality, and the physical plane is at the centre: it is like a screen on which all the intervening vibrations are projected and held, as upon a screen—it is an image, an image of all that is happening. We notice it because it is a thing done, something concrete. It is as though you viewed the whole universe as a movement of force and this movement of force were projected till it met a screen and on the screen it made an image, and this image on the screen is the physical world. And it is a mere image. The physical world which everyone takes as the only reality is simply an image. It is the image of all that happens in what we call the invisible. It becomes visible to us because there is a screen which intervenes and stops the vibrations and that produces an image. If there were no such screen the vibrations would move on and nothing would be seen. And yet all the movements would exist. But for us they would be invisible, if there were no screen to stop the vibrations.

For the ordinary consciousness it is the image alone that is true and what happens behind it is more or less problematical, but in the true consciousness, all that happens behind or before is the true thing and what one sees externally is only an image, that is to say, a projection on a screen, of something which exists altogether independently. So, our body represents a small fragment in this set of images that is projected and it is a fragment which expresses exactly all the vibrations of the inner state corresponding to this little point that is the body. (5-272,273)

To Know Oneself Integrally Requires a Personal Commitment to Life

This depends upon the attitude your friend has taken in life. If he wants to be a sadhak,[2] it is indispensable that rules of ordinary morality do not have any value for him. Now, if he is an ordinary man living the ordinary life, it is a purely practical question, isn't it? He must conform to the laws of the country in which he lives to avoid all trouble! But all these things which in ordinary life have a very relative value and can be looked upon with a certain indulgence, change totally the minute one decides to do yoga and enter the divine life. Then, all values change completely; what is honest in ordinary life, is no longer at all honest for you. Besides, there is such a reversal of values that one can no longer use the same ordinary language. If one wants to consecrate oneself to the divine life, one must do it truly, that is, give oneself entirely, no longer do anything for one's own interest, depend exclusively upon the divine Power to which one abandons oneself. Everything changes completely, doesn't it?—everything, everything, it is a reversal. What I have just read from this book applies solely to those who want to do yoga; for others it has no meaning, it is a language which makes no sense, but for those who want to do yoga it is imperative. It is always the same thing in all that we have recently read: one must be careful not to have one foot on one side and the other foot on the other, not to bestride two different boats each following its own course. This is what Sri Aurobindo said: one must not lead a "double life". One must give up one thing or the other—one can't follow both.

This does not mean, however, that one is obliged to get out of the conditions of one's life: it is the inner attitude which must be totally changed. One may do what one is in the habit of doing, but do it with quite a different attitude. I don't say it is necessary to give up everything in life and go away into solitude, to an ashram necessarily, to do yoga. Now, it is true that if one does yoga in the world and in worldly circumstances, it is more difficult, but it is also more complete. Because, every minute one must face problems which do not present themselves. (4-378)

Evolution to Self-Awareness

Nature is not consciously intelligent? . . .

There is an intelligence which acts in her and through her, in her action, but she is not conscious of this intelligence. You can understand this with animals. Take ants, for example. They do exactly what they have to do; all their work and organisation is something which really looks perfect. But they are not conscious of the intelligence which organises them. They are moved mechanically by an intelligence of which they are not aware. And even if you take the most developed animals, like the cat and dog for instance, they know exactly what they have to do: a cat bringing up its little ones brings them up just as well as a woman hers—sometimes better than a woman but it is impelled by an intelligence which moves it automatically. It is not conscious of the intelligence which makes it do things. It is not aware of it, it cannot change anything at all in the movement by its own will. Something makes it act mechanically but over that it has no control.

If a human being intervenes and trains a cat, he can make it change its behaviour; but it is the consciousness of the human being which acts upon it, not its own consciousness. It is not conscious of the intelligence which makes it act.

And this kind of self-awareness, this possibility of watching oneself acting, of understanding why one does things, how one does them and, therefore, of having a control and changing the action—that belongs to the mind and in his own right to man. This is the essential difference between a man and an animal—that a man is conscious of himself, that he can become aware of the force which makes him act, and not only become aware of it but control it.

But all those who feel themselves driven by a force and say, "I was forced to do it", without the participation of their will, show that they are still deeply rooted in animality, that is to say, in the inconscient. One begins to become a conscious human being only when one knows why one does things and when one is capable of changing one's action by a determined will, when one has a control. Before having any control, one is still more or less an animal with a small embryo of consciousness which is just beginning, a little flame flickering and trying to burn, and likely to be blown out by the slightest passing breeze. (8-60,61)

Who Am I?

Sweet Mother, if there is someone who wants to have experiences or something like that, what is the first thing he should do?

To have experiences? What kind of experiences? Have visions or have psychological experiences or—what kind of experiences?

In fact, the whole life is an experience, isn't it? We spend our time having experiences. You mean having a contact with other realities than physical ones? Is it that? Ah!

Well, I think the first consideration is to have, to begin with, the faith that there is something other than the physical reality. This can be the first condition. Then the second condition is to try to find what it is, and the best field of action is oneself. So one must begin by studying oneself a little, and manage to discern between what depends exclusively on the body and what on something else which is not the body. One can begin like that. One can begin by observing one's feelings or thoughts in their working; because . . . sensations are so linked to the body that it is very novices were given an image when they were invested with the white robe; they were told: "Do not try to remove the stains one by one, the whole robe must be purified." Do not try to correct your faults one by one, to overcome your weaknesses one by one, it does not take you very far. The entire consciousness must be changed, a reversal of consciousness must be achieved, a springing up out of the state in which one is towards a higher state from which one dominates all the weaknesses one wants to heal, and from which one has a full vision of the work to be accomplished.

I believe Sri Aurobindo has said this: things are such that it may be said that nothing is done until everything is done. One step ahead is not enough, a total conversion is necessary.

How many times have I heard people who were making an effort say, "I try, but what's the use of my trying? Every time I think I have gained something, I find that I must begin all over again." This happens because they are trying to go forward while standing still, they are trying to progress without changing their consciousness. It is the entire point of view which must be shifted, the whole consciousness must get out of the rut in which it lies so as to rise up and see things from above. It is only thus that victories will not be changed into defeats.

Anything else? No, nothing more?

Mother, how to change one's consciousness?

Naturally, there are many ways, but each person must do it by the means accessible to him; and the indication of the way usually comes spontaneously, through something like an unexpected experience. And for each one, it appears a little differently.

For instance, one may have the perception of the ordinary consciousness which is extended on the surface, horizontally, and works on a plane which is simultaneously the surface of things and has a contact with the superficial outer side of things, people, circumstances; and then, suddenly, for some reason or other—as I say for each one it is different—there is a shifting upwards, and instead of seeing things horizontally, of being at the same level as they are, you suddenly dominate them and see them from above, in their totality, instead of seeing a small number of things immediately next to yourself; it is as though something were drawing you above and making you see as from a mountain-top or an aeroplane. And instead of seeing each detail and seeing it on its own level, you see the whole as one unit, and from far above.

There are many ways of having this experience, but it usually comes to you as if by chance, one fine day.

Or else, one may have an experience which is almost its very opposite but which comes to the same thing. Suddenly one plunges into a depth, one moves away from the thing one perceived, it seems distant, superficial, unimportant; one enters an inner silence or an inner calm or an inward vision of things, a profound feeling, a more intimate perception of circumstances and things, in which all values change. And one becomes aware of a sort of unity, a deep identity which is one in spite of the diverse appearances.

Or else, suddenly also, the sense of limitation disappears and one enters the perception of a kind of indefinite duration beginningless and endless, or something which has always been and always be.

These experiences come to you suddenly in a flash, for a second, a moment in your life, you don't know why or how. . . . There are other ways, other experiences—they are innumerable, they vary according to people; but with this, with one minute, one second of such an existence, one catches the tail of the thing. So one must remember that, try to relive it, go to the depths of the experience, recall it, aspire, concentrate. This is the starting-point, the end of the guiding thread, the clue. For all those who are destined to find their inner being, the truth of their being, there is always at least one moment in life when they were no longer the same, perhaps just like a lightning-flash—but that is enough. It indicates the road one should take, it is the door that opens on this path. And so you must pass through the door, and with perseverance and an unfailing steadfastness seek to renew the state which will lead you to something more real and more total.

Many ways have always been given, but a way you have been taught, a way you have read about in books or heard from a teacher, does not have the effective value of a spontaneous experience which has come without any apparent reason, and which is simply the blossoming of the soul's awakening, one second contact with your psychic being[4] which shows you the best way for you, the one most within your reach, which you will then have to follow with perseverance to reach the goal—one second which shows you how to start, the beginning. . . . Some have this in dreams at night; some have it at odd times: something one sees which awakens in one this new consciousness, something one hears, a beautiful landscape, beautiful music, or else simply a few words one reads, or else the intensity of concentration in some effort—anything at all, there are a thousand reasons and thousands of ways of having it. But, I repeat, all those who are destined to realise have had this at least once in one's life. It may be very fleeting, it may have come when they were very young, but always at least once in one's life one has the experience of what true consciousness is. Well, that is the best indication of the path to be followed.

One may seek within oneself, one may remember, may observe; one must notice what is going on, one must pay attention, that's all. Sometimes, when one sees a generous act, hears of something exceptional, when one witnesses heroism or generosity or greatness of soul, meets someone who shows a special talent or acts in an exceptional and beautiful way, there is a kind of enthusiasm or admiration or gratitude which suddenly awakens in the being and opens the door to a state, a new state of consciousness, a light, a warmth, a joy one did not know before. That too is a way of catching the guiding thread. There are a thousand ways, one has only to be awake and to watch.

First of all, you must feel the necessity for this change of consciousness, accept the idea that it is this, the path which must lead to the goal; and once you admit the principle, you must be watchful. And you will find, you do find it. And once you have found it, you must start walking without any hesitation.

Indeed, the starting-point is to observe oneself, not to live in a perpetual nonchalance, a perpetual apathy; one must be attentive. (8-402,403,404,405)

Changing Our Habits

Is it the same thing, the same work, to be conscious that the nature must be changed and to master the different parts of the being?

One precedes the other. First of all one must be conscious, then control, and by continuing the mastery one changes one's character. Changing the character is what comes last. One must control bad habits, the old habits, for a very long time for them to drop off and the character to change.

We may take the example of someone who has frequent depressions. When things are not exactly as he would like them to be, he becomes depressed. So, to begin with, he must become aware of his depression—not only of the depression but of the causes of depression, why he gets depressed so easily. Then, once he has become conscious, he must master the depressions, must stop being depressed even when the cause of depression is there—he must master his depression, stop it from coming. And finally, after his work has been done for a sufficiently long time, the nature loses the habit of having depressions and no longer reacts in the same way, the nature is changed. (4-341,342)

Cleansing Our Subconscious Mind

> *"The subconscient is the main cause why all things repeat themselves and nothing ever gets changed except in appearance. It is the cause why people say character cannot be changed, the cause also of the constant return of things one hoped to have got rid of for ever. . . . All too that is suppressed without being wholly got rid of sinks down there and remains as seed ready to surge up or sprout up at any moment."*
>
> Bases of Yoga

But it is not hopeless, because if it were hopeless never could we attain physical transformation.

There.

Now, questions.

Sweet Mother, how should we reject something in the vital so that it doesn't enter the subconscient?

Ah!

There is a great difference between pushing back a thing simply because one doesn't want it and changing the state of one's consciousness which makes the thing totally foreign to one's nature. Usually, when one has a movement one doesn't want, one drives it away or pushes it back, but one doesn't take the precaution of finding within oneself what has served and still serves as a support for this movement, the particular tendency, the fold of consciousness which enables this thing to enter the consciousness. If, on the contrary, instead of simply making a movement of reprobation and rejection, one enters deeply into his vital consciousness and finds the support, that is, a kind of particular little vibration buried very deeply in a corner, often in such a dark corner that it is difficult to find it there; if one starts hunting it down, that is, if one goes within, concentrates, follows as it were the trail of this movement to its origin, one finds something like a very tiny serpent coiled up, something at times quite tiny, not bigger than a pea, but very black and sunk very deeply.

And then there are two methods: either to put so intense a light, the light of a truth-consciousness so strong, that this will be dissolved; or else to catch the thing as with pincers, pull it out from its place and hold it up before one's consciousness. The first method is radical but one doesn't always have at his disposal this light of truth, so one can't always use it. The second method can be taken, but it hurts, it hurts as badly as the extraction of a tooth; I don't know if you have ever had a tooth pulled out, but it hurts as much as that, and it hurts here, like that. (*Mother shows the centre of the chest and makes a movement of twisting.*) And usually one is not very courageous. When it hurts very much, well, one tries to efface it like this (*gesture*) and that is why things persist. But if one has the courage to take hold of it and pull it until it comes out and to put it before himself, even if it hurts very much . . . to hold it up like this (*gesture*) until one can see it clearly, and then dissolve it, then it is finished. The thing will never again hide in the subconscient and will never again return to bother you. But this is a radical operation. It must be done like an operation.

You must first have a great deal of perseverence in the search, for usually when one begins searching for these things the mind comes to give a hundred and one favourable explanations for your not needing to search. It tells you, "Why no, it is not at all your fault; it is this, it is that, it is the circumstances, it is the people, these are things received from outside—all kinds of excellent excuses, which, unless you are very firm in your resolution, make you let go, and then it is finished; and so, after a short time the whole business has to be started again, the bad impulse or the thing you didn't want, the movement you didn't want, comes back, and so you must begin everything over again—till the day you decide to perform the operation. When the operation is done it is over, one is free. But, as I said, you must distrust mental explanations, because each time one says, "Yes, yes, at other times it was like that, but this time truly, truly it is not my fault, it is not my fault." There you are. So it is finished. You must begin again. The subconscient is there, the thing goes down, remains there, very comfortably, and the first day you are not on your guard, hop! it surges up again and it can last—I knew people for whom it lasted more than thirty-five years, because they did not resolve even once to do what was necessary.

Yes, it hurts, it hurts a little, that's all; afterwards it is finished. So there we are. (7-83,84,85)

On Speech and Telling Lies

Try this little exercise: at the beginning of the day, say: "I won't speak without thinking of what I say." You believe, don't you, that you think all that you say! It is not at all true, you will see that so many times the word you do not want to say is ready to come out, and that you are compelled to make a conscious effort to stop it from coming out.

I have known people who were very scrupulous about not telling lies, but all of a sudden, when together in a group, instead of speaking the truth they would spontaneously tell a lie; they did not have the intention of doing so, they did not think of it a minute before doing it, but it came "like that". Why?—because they were in the company of liars; there was an atmosphere of falsehood and they had quite simply caught the malady!

It is thus that gradually, slowly, with perseverance, first of all with great care and much attention, one becomes conscious, learns to know oneself and then to become master of oneself. (4-36,37)

Our Love for Progress

"It is only by observing these movements (of our being) with great care, by bringing them, as it were, before the tribunal of our highest ideal, with a sincere will to submit

to its judgment, that we can hope to educate in us a discernment which does not err."

"The Science of Living", *On Education*

One must be clearly aware of the origin of one's movements because there are contradictory velleities in the being—some pushing you here, others pushing you there, and that obviously creates chaos in life. If you observe yourself, you will see that as soon as you do something which disturbs you a little, the mind immediately gives you a favourable reason to justify yourself—this mind is capable of gilding everything. In these conditions it is difficult to know oneself. One must be absolutely sincere to be able to do it and to see clearly into all the little falsehoods of the mental being.

If in your mind you go over the various movements and reactions of the day like one repeating indefinitely the same thing, you will not progress. If this reviewing is to make you progress, you must find something within you in whose light you can be yourself your own judge, something which represents for you the best part of yourself, which has some light, some goodwill and which precisely is in love with progress. Place that before you and first, pass across it as in a cinema all that you have done, all that you have felt, your impulses, your thoughts, etc.; then try to coordinate them, that is, find out why this has followed that. And look at the luminous screen that is before you: certain things pass by well, without throwing a shadow; others, on the contrary, throw a little shadow; others yet cast a shadow altogether black and disagreeable. You must do this very sincerely, as though you were playing a game: under such circumstances I did such and such a thing, feeling like this and thinking in this way; I have before me my ideal of knowledge and self-mastery, well, was this act in keeping with my ideal or not? If it was, it would not leave any shadow on the screen, which would remain transparent, and one would not have to worry about it. If it is not in conformity, it casts a shadow. Why has it left this shadow? What was there in this act that was contrary to the will to self-knowledge and self-mastery? Most often you will find that it corresponds to unconsciousness—then you file it among unconscious things and resolve that next time you will try to be conscious before doing anything. But in other cases you will see that it was a nasty little egoism, quite black, which had come to distort your action or your thought. Then you place this egoism before your "light" and ask yourself: "Why has it the right to make me act like that, think like that? . . ." And instead of accepting any odd explanation you must search and you will find a corner of your being something which thinks and says, "Ah, no, I shall accept everything but that." You will see that it is a petty vanity, a movement of self-love, an egoistic feeling hidden somewhere, a hundred things. Then you take a good look at these things in the light of your ideal: "Is cherishing this movement in conformity with my seeking and the realisation of my ideal or not? I put this little dark corner in front of the light until the light enters into it and it disappears." Then the comedy is over. But the comedy of your whole day is not finished yet, you know, for there are many things which have to pass thus before the light. But if you continue this game—for truly it is a game, if you do this sincerely—I assure you that in six months you will not recognise yourself, you will say to yourself, "What? I was like that! It is impossible!"

You may be five years old or twenty, fifty or sixty and transform yourself in this way by putting everything before this inner light. You will see that the elements which do not conform with your ideal are not generally elements which you have to throw wholly out of yourself (there are very few of this kind); they are simply things not in their place. If you organise everything—your feelings, your thoughts, your impulses, etc.—around the psychic centre which is the inner light, you will see that all inner disorder will change into a luminous order.

It is quite evident that if a similar procedure were

adopted by a nation or by the earth, most of the things which make men unhappy would disappear, for the major part of the world's misery comes from the fact that things are not in their place. If life were organised in such a way that nothing was wasted and each thing was in its place, most of these miseries would not exist any longer. An old sage has said:

"There is no evil. There is only a lack of balance.

"There is nothing bad. Only things are not in their place."

If everything were in its place, in nations, in the material world, in the actions and thoughts and feelings of individuals, the greater part of human suffering would disappear.

There are two things to be considered: consciousness and the instruments through which consciousness manifests. Let us take the instruments through which consciousness manifests. Let us take the instruments: there is the mental being which produces thoughts, the emotional being which produces feeling, the vital being which produces the power of action and the physical being that acts.

The man of genius may use anything at all and make something beautiful because he has genius; but give this genius a perfect instrument and he will make something wonderful. Take a great musician; well, even with a wretched piano and missing notes, he will produce something beautiful; but give him a good piano, well-tuned, and he will do something still more beautiful. The consciousness is the same in either case but for expression it needs a good instrument—a body with mental, vital, psychic and physical capacities. (4-38,39,40)

At Times It Is Necessary to Pull Back From Identification with Our Surface Movements

What is the meaning of "the mental witness"?

The witness we have spoken about several times already, only here it is in the mind.

There are witnesses everywhere. It is a capacity of the being to detach itself, to stand back and look at what is happening, as when one looks at something happening in the street or when one looks at others playing and does not himself play, one remains seated, looking at the others moving but does not move. That's how it is.

In all the parts of the being there is one side which can do this: put itself at the back, remain quiet and look, without participating. This is what is called the witness. One has many witnesses inside onself, and often one is a witness without even being aware of it. And if you develop this, it always gives you the possibility of being quiet and not being affect by things. One detaches oneself from them, looks at them as at a dramatic scene, without participating in it. This does not change things very much. (6-426)

Sweet Mother, what does "the reduction of the mental being to the position of a witness" mean?

Have you never felt this? As though you were a little behind or above things, and were looking at them taking place but were not doing anything yourself? Witness means an observer, someone who looks on and does not act himself. So, when the mind is very quiet, one can withdraw a little in this way from circumstances and look at things as though he were a witness, a spectator, and not participating in the action himself. This gives you a great detachment, a great quietude, and also a very precise sense of the value of things, because it cuts the attachment to action. When you know how to do this with yourself, when you can withdraw and watch yourself acting, you learn many things about yourself. When you are all mixed up and take part in the action, you do not observe yourself acting, you don't know what you are like. But when you draw back and look at yourself, you can perceive many imperfections which you wouldn't have seen otherwise. (6-360)

The Interplay of Forces—Thoughts, Feelings, Desires

But then what is mental and vital will?

That is an expression of something which is not personal.

If you analyse carefully, you see, for instance, that all that you think has been thought by others, that these are things which circulate and pass through you, but you have not produced this thought, you are not the originator of this thought. All your reactions come from atavism, from those who gave you birth and from the environment in which you have lived, from all the impressions which have accumulated in you and constituted something which seems to you yourself, yet which is not produced by you, but merely felt and experienced; you become aware of it in passing, but it is not you who created it, not you who gave it birth.

It could be said that these are like sounds—any kind of sounds: words, music, anything—recorded by an instrument, then reproduced by another instrument which plays them back like a gramophone, for instance. You wouldn't say that the gramophone has created the sound you hear, would you? That would never occur to you. But as you are under the illusion of your separate personality, these thoughts which cross your mind and find expression, these feelings which pass through your vital and find expression, you think, have come from you; but nothing comes from you. Where is the "you" which can create all that?

You must go deep, deep within, and find the eternal essence of your being to know the creative reality in yourself. And once you have found that, you will realise that it is one single thing, the same in all others, and so where is your separate personality? Nothing's left any longer.

Yes, these are recording and reproducing instruments, and there are always what might be called distortions—they may be distortions for the better, they may be distortions for the worse, they may be fairly great changes; the inner combinations are such that things are not reproduced exactly as they passed from one to the other because the instrument is very complex. But it is one and the same thing which is moved by a conscious will, quite independent of all personal wills.

When the Buddha wanted to make his disciples understand these things, he used to tell them: every time you send out a vibration, a desire for example, the desire for some particular thing, your desire starts circulating from one person to another, from one to another across the universe and will go right round and come back to you. And as it is not only one thing but a world of things, and as you are not the only transmitting centre—all individuals are transmitting centres—it is such a confusion that you lose your bearings in there. But these vibrations move about in a single, absolutely identical field; it is only the complication and interception of the vibrations which give you the impression of something independent or separate.

But there's nothing separate or independent; there is only *one* Substance, *one* Force, *one* Consciousness, *one* Will, which moves in countless ways of being.

And it is so complicated that one is no longer aware of it, but if one steps back and follows the movement, no matter which line of movement, one can see very clearly that the vibrations propagate themselves, one following another, one following another, one following another, and that in fact there is only one unity—unity of Substance, unity of Consciousness, unity of Will. And that is the only reality. Outwardly there is a kind of illusion: the illusion of separation and the illusion of difference.

Desires and all those things also?

This is not personal. Not at all personal. And that is *very* easy to find out; of all things this is the easiest to discern, because ninety times out of a hundred it comes to you from someone else or from a certain circumstance or a set of circumstances, or from a vibration coming from another person or several other people. It is very easy to discern, it is the first thing one can discern: it is a vibration which suddenly awakens something similar in you. You know, something makes an impact on you, and this impact brings up a response, as when you play a note. Well, this vibration of desire comes and strikes you in a certain way and you respond.

It is not very difficult to discern; even when one is very young, even when one is a child, if one pays attention, one becomes aware of this. One lives amidst constant collective suggestions, constantly; for example, I don't know if you have been present at funerals, or if you have been in a house where someone has died—naturally you must observe yourself a little, otherwise you won't notice anything—but if you observe yourself a little, you will see that you had no special reason to feel any sorrow or grief whatever for the passing away of this person; he is a person like many others; this has happened and by a combination of social circumstances you have come to that house. And there, suddenly, without knowing why or how, you feel a strong emotion, a great sorrow, a deep pain, and you ask yourself, "Why am I so unhappy?" It is quite simply the vibrations which have entered you, nothing else.

And I tell you it is easy to observe, for it is an experience I had when I was a little child—and at that time I was not yet doing conscious yoga; perhaps I was doing yoga but not consciously—and I observed it very, very clearly. I told myself, "Surely it is their sorrow I am feeling, for I have no reason to be specially affected by this person's death"; and all of a sudden, tears came to my eyes, I felt as though a lump were in my throat and I wanted to cry, as though I were in great sorrow—I was a small child—and immediately I understood, "Oh! it is their sorrow which has come inside me."

It is the same thing for anger. It is very clear, one receives it suddenly, not even from a person, from the atmosphere—it is there—and then all of a sudden it enters you and usually it gets hold of you from below and then rises up and pushes you, and so off you go. A minute earlier you were not angry, you were quite self-possessed, you had no intention of losing your temper. And this seizes you so strongly that you can't resist—because you are not sufficiently conscious, you let it enter you . . . that is to say, your body. (8-51,52,53,54)

Emerging from Our Egocentric Shell to the Vastness of the Universe

Sweet Mother, how can we make our consciousness vast?

Vast? Ah, there are many ways of doing this.

The easiest way is to identify yourself with something vast. For instance, when you feel that you are shut up in a completely narrow and limited thought, will, consciousness, when you feel as though you were in a shell, then if you begin thinking about something very vast, as for example, the immensity of the waters of an ocean, and if really you can think of this ocean and how it stretches out far, far, far, far, in all directions, like this (Mother stretches out her arms), how, compared with you, it is so far, so far that you cannot see the other shore, you cannot reach its end anywhere, neither behind or in front nor to the right or left . . . it is wide, wide, wide, wide . . . you think of this and then you feel that you are floating on this sea, like that, and there are no limits. . . . This is very easy. Then you can widen your consciousness a little.

Other people, for example, begin looking at the sky; and then they imagine all those spaces between all those stars, and all . . . that kind of infinity of spaces in which the earth is a tiny point, and you too are just a very tiny point, smaller than an ant, on the earth. And so you look at the sky and feel that you are floating in these infinite spaces between the planets, and that you are growing vaster and vaster to go farther and farther. Some people succeed with this.

There is a way also by trying to identify yourself with all things upon earth. For example, when you have a small narrow vision of something and are hurt by others' vision and point of view, you must begin by shifting your consciousness, try to put it in others, and try gradually to identify yourself with all the different ways of thinking of all others. This is a little more . . . how shall I put it? . . . dangerous. Because to identify oneself with the thought and will of others means to identify oneself with a heap of stupidities (*Mother laughs*) and bad wills, and this may bring consequences which are not very good. But still, some people do this more easily. For instance, when they are in disagreement with someone, in order to widen their consciousness they try to put themselves in the place of the other and see the things not from their own point of view but from the point of view of the other. This widens the consciousness, though not as much as by the first ways I spoke about, which are quite innocent. They don't do you any harm, they do you much good. They make you very peaceful.

There are lots of intellectual ways of widening the consciousness. These I have explained fully in my book. But in any case, when you are bored by something, when something is painful to you or very unpleasant, if you begin to think of the eternity of time and the immensity of space, if you think of all that has gone before and all that will come afterwards, and that this second in eternity is truly just a passing breath, and that it seems so utterly ridiculous to be upset by something which in the eternity of times is . . . one doesn't even have the time to become aware of it, it has no place, no importance, because, what indeed is a second in eternity? If one can manage to realise that, to . . . how to put it? . . . visualise, picture the little person one is, in the little earth where one is, and the tiny second of consciousness which for the moment is hurting you or is unpleasant for you, just this—which in itself is only a second in your existence, and that you yourself have been many things before and will be many more things afterwards, that what affects you now you will have probably completely forgotten in ten years, or if you remember it you will say, "How did I happen to attach any importance to that?" . . . if you can realise that first and then realise your little person which is a second in eternity, not even a second, you know, imperceptible, a fragment of a second in eternity, that the whole world has unrolled before this and will unroll yet, indefinitely—before, behind—and that . . . well, then suddenly you sense the utter ridiculousness of the importance you attach to what happened to you. . . . *Truly* you feel . . . to what an extent it is absurd to attach any importance to one's life, to oneself, and to what happens to you. And in the space of three minutes, if you do this properly, all unpleasantness is swept away. Even a very deep pain can be swept away. Simply a concentration like this, and to place oneself in infinity and eternity. Everything goes away. One comes out of it cleansed. One can get rid of *all* attachments and even, I say, of the deepest sorrows—of everything, in this way—if one knows how to do it in the right way. It immediately takes you out of your little ego. (6-344,345,346)

To Be A Conscious Being One Must Have A Unified Will

The breath has passed, you see. You don't know . . . something . . . a moment of unconsciousness . . . "Oh, I was not conscious." You are not conscious because you do not accept . . . And all this because one doesn't know how to will.

To learn how to will is a very important thing. And to will truly, you must unify your being. In fact, to be a being, one must first unify oneself. If one is pulled by absolutely opposite tendencies, if one spends three-fourths of his life without being conscious of himself and the reasons why he does things, is one a real being? One does not exist. One is a mass of influences, movements, forces, actions, reactions, but one is not a being. One begins to become a being when he begins to have a will. And one can't have a will unless he is unified.

And when you have a will, you will be able to say, say to the Divine: "I want what You want." But not before that. Because in order to want what the Divine wants, you must have a will, otherwise you can will nothing at all. You would like to. You would like it very much. You would very much like to want what the Divine wants to do. You don't possess a will to give to Him and to put at His service. Something like that, gelatinous, like jelly-fish . . . there . . . a mass of good wills—and I am considering the better side of things and forgetting the bad wills—a mass of good wills, half-conscious and fluctuating. . . . (6-348)

To Know the Divine Will

But it is difficult to know the divine Will, isn't it?

We have already studied the subject at length. Don't you remember what we said? There are four conditions for knowing the divine Will:

The first essential condition: an absolute sincerity.

Second: To overcome desires and preferences.

Third: To silence the mind and listen.

Fourth: To obey immediately when you receive the order.

If you persist you will perceive the divine Will more and more clearly. But even before you know what it is, you can make an offering of your own will and you will see that all circumstances will be so arranged as to make you do the right thing. But you must not be like that person I knew who used to say, "I always see the divine Will in others." That can land you anywhere, there is nothing more dangerous, for if you think you see the divine Will in others, you are sure to do their will, not the divine Will. There too we can say that not one among many, many human beings acts in accord with the divine Will. (4-208)

Lack of Integration between One's Work and Personal Life

When one reads ordinary books, one has the impression of entering into the mind of the author and that is not always pleasant. I have also noticed that when one talks about business or work with an outsider, the conversation can be good and interesting, but as soon as one talks with the same person about his private life, the conversation immediately becomes painful.

Yes, because work, especially if it is technical work, is the expression of the best in the man, while in his private life he comes down to a lower level, with very few exceptions. So many remarkable scholars, writers, artists who produce remarkable things, once they enter their homes, become detestable husbands, unpleasant fathers, intolerable people for those who are around them. And I am speaking of an elite, those who make special studies, discoveries, who run big institutions: outside, they are uncommon people, men of great abilities; back home they become commonplace and often unbearable—they have a nice time, they take rest, relax themselves. And if they begin to amuse themselves, that's the end of it all! I knew people of great intelligence, admirable artists who, as soon as they began to "relax", became utterly foolish! They did the most vulgar things, behaved like ill-bred children—they were relaxing. Everything comes from this "need" of relaxation; and what does that mean for most men? It means, always, coming down to a lower level. They do not know that for a true relaxation one must rise one degree higher, one must rise above oneself. If one goes down, it adds to one's fatigue and brings a stupefaction. Besides, each time one comes down, one increases the load of the subconscient—this huge subconscient load which one must clean and clean if one wants to mount, and which is like fetters on the feet. But it is difficult to teach that, for one must know it oneself before one can teach it to others.

This is never told to children, they are allowed to commit all the stupidities in the world under the pretext that they need relaxation.

It is not by sinking below oneself that one removes fatigue. One must climb the ladder and there one has true rest, because one has the inner peace, the light, the universal energy. And little by little one puts oneself in touch with the truth which is the very reason of one's existence.

If you contact that definitively, it removes completely all fatigue. (4-155,156)

Trust Only the Divine

. . . but there is one thing you must learn, never to rely on anyone or anything whatever except the Divine. For if you lean upon anyone for support, that support will break, you may be sure of that. From the minute you start doing yoga (I always speak of those who do yoga, I do not speak about ordinary life), for those who do yoga, to depend upon someone else is like wanting to transform that person into a representative of the Divine Force; now you may be sure there is not one in a hundred millions who can carry the weight: he will break immediately. So never take the attitude of hoping for support, help, comfort from anyone except the Divine. That is absolute; I have never, not once, met anyone who tried to cling to something to find a support there (someone doing yoga or who has been put into touch with yoga) and who was not deceived—it breaks, it stops, one loses one's support. Then one says, "Life is difficult"—it is not difficult but one must know what one is doing.

Never seek a support elsewhere than in the Divine. Never seek satisfaction elsewhere than in the Divine. Never seek the satisfaction of your needs in anyone else except the Divine—never, for anything at all. All your needs can be satisfied only by the Divine. All your weaknesses can be borne and healed only by the Divine. He alone is capable of giving you what you need in everything, always, and if you try to find any satisfaction or support or help or joy or . . . Heaven knows what, in anyone else, you will always fall on your nose one day, and that always hurts, sometimes even hurts very much. (4-391)

Notes to Chapter 1

[1] Tomb of Sri Aurobindo.

[2] A practitioner of yoga which is a method of inquiry into one's fundamental root of existence.

[3] Agni is the Divine Will in the center of our being.

[4] Similar to the soul but there is a distinction. The psychic being is the eternal spark of the Divine within us but is in a continual state of formation as a result of our life's experiences.

2

INDIVIDUALIZATION

What does it mean to become an individual? At what point are we a complete, fulfilled human being? This chapter explores some of the issues regarding our sense of individuality and the role of the ego. If we should be so fortunate to attain the status of an "individual," are we finished? This chapter will show us the way to an ultimate completion.

The Three Stages of Individuality

> *What is it? "For our entire nature and its environment, all our personal and all our universal self, are full of habits and of influences that are opposed to our spiritual rebirth. . . "*

Our universal self is our relation with all others and all the movements of Nature.

And I have often told you, haven't I?, that the first state of your being is a state of an almost total mixture with all things from outside, and that there is almost no individualisation, that is, specialisation which makes you a different being. You are moved—a kind of form which is your physical being is moved—by all the common universal forces, vital forces or mental forces, which go through your form and put it in motion.

So that is the universal being.

And all that you have wrested from this general semiconsciousness, and have crystallised into a more or less independent being, conscious of itself and having its own qualities, all this is your individual being. And this individual being is full of all the movements of obscurity, unconsciousness, and of the limitations of ordinary life, and that's . . . and that's what you must gradually open to the divine influence and bring to the consciousness and understanding of things. That's what Sri Aurobindo says.

In fact, the first victory is to create an individuality. And then later, the second victory is to give this individuality to the Divine. And the third victory is that the Divine changes your individuality into a divine being.

There are three stages: the first is to become an individual; the second is to consecrate the individual, that he may surrender entirely to the Divine and be identified with Him; and the third is that the Divine takes possession of this individual and changes him into a being in His own image, that is, he too becomes divine.

Generally, all the yogas stopped at the second. (7-407)

Defining One's Individuality

Sweet Mother, why are we so attached to our ego?

As I said just now, probably because you still need it very much, isn't that so? In order to become a conscious, individualised being, one needs his ego; that is why it is there. It is only when one has realised his own individuality sufficiently, has become a conscious, independent being with its own reality, that he no longer needs the ego. And at that time one can make an effort to get rid of it. Unfortunately most people, as soon as they become real individuals, have such a sense of their importance and their ability that they no longer even think at all of getting rid of their ego. But that of course is something else.

Here I don't let you go to sleep. I remind you from time to time of the true thing. But you are all very young, you see, and a certain number of years are *needed*, years of intensive inner formation, to become a being who thinks for himself, is conscious of his own will, and conscious of his own nature, his purpose of existence, independent of human mass. A certain time is necessary. Some children begin when *very small*. If one begins very early, when one is twenty he can be quite formed. But you must begin when very small, and consciously, very consciously; you must begin with a sense of observation of all the movements in yourself, of their relation with others, of—precisely, of your degree of independence, real individuality, of knowing where impulses come from, where other movements come from: whether it is contagion from outside or something that arises from within yourself. A very profound study of all the movements in oneself is necessary in order to succeed simply in crystallising a being who is a little conscious, *a little* conscious. But when you live fluidly, so to say, when you don't even know what goes on inside you, have some sort of vague impressions, if you question yourself, at least ninety-nine times out of a hundred, if you ask yourself, "Why did I think like that? Why did I feel like that?", even "Why did I do that?", then the reply is almost always the same: "I don't know. It came like that, that's all." That is to say, one is not at all conscious.

Are you able to know, when you are with others, what comes from you and what from the others? to what extent their way of being, their particular vibrations act upon you? You are not aware of this at all. You live in a kind of "approximate" consciousness, half-awake, half-asleep, in something very vague, where you have to grope like this in order to catch things. But do you have a precise, clear, exact notion of what goes on in you, why it goes on in you? And then, this: the vibrations which come to you from outside and those which come from within you? And then, again, what can come from others, changing all this, giving another orientation? You live in a kind of hazy fluidity, certain small things suddenly crystallize in your consciousness, you have just caught them for a moment; and it is just clear enough like that, as though there was a projector, just something passing on the screen and becoming clear for a second: the next minute everything has become vague, imprecise, but you are not aware of this because you have not even asked yourself the question, because you live in this way. It stops here, begins here, ends here. That's all. You do from day to day, minute to minute, things which you do, like that . . . it happens to be like that.

It will come. It will come. Surely it will come. I am not going to leave you like that. . . . Shake you up a little—I am going to shake you up a little. I shall do what is necessary for this. (6-334,335,336)

The Ego and Individuality

When the vast majority of people say "I", it is a part of them, of their feeling, their body, their thought, indifferently, which speaks; it is something that always changes. Therefore, their "I" is innumerable, or the "I" always varies. What is the constant thing therein? . . . The psychic being, evidently. For, to be constant a thing must first be immortal. Otherwise it cannot be constant. Then, it must also be independent of the experiences through which it passes: it cannot be the experiences themselves. Hence, it is certainly not the bed of the river which constitutes the river; the bed is only a circumstance. If the comparison is carried a little farther (besides, comparisons are worthless, people find in them whatever they want), it can be said that the river is a good symbol of life, that what is constant in the river is the species "water". It is not always the same drop of water, but it is always water—without water there would be no river. And what endures in the human being is the species "consciousness". It is because it has a consciousness that it endures. It is not the forms which last, it is the consciousness, the power of binding together all these forms, of passing through all these things, not only keeping a memory of them (memory is something very external), but keeping the same vibration of consciousness.

And that is the great mystery of creation, for it is the same consciousness, the Consciousness is one. But the very moment this Consciousness manifests itself, exteriorises itself, deploys itself, it divides itself into innumerable fragments for the need of expansion, and each one of these fragmentations has been the beginning, the origin of an individual being. The origin of every individual form is the law of this form or the truth of this form. If there were no law, no truth of each form, there would be no possibility of individualisation. It would be something extending indefinitely; there would be perhaps points of concentration, assemblages, but no individual consciousness. Each form then represents one element in the changing of the One into the many. This multiplicity implies an innumerable quantity of laws, elements of consciousness, truths which spread out into the universe and finally become separate individualities. So the individual being seems constantly to go farther and farther away from its origin by the very necessity of individualisation. But once this individualisation, that is, this awareness of the inner truth is complete, it becomes possible, by an inner identification, to re-establish in the multiplicity the original unity; that is the *raison d'être* of the universe as we perceive it. The universe has been made so that this phenomenon may take place. The Supreme has manifested Himself to Himself so as to become aware of Himself.

In any case, that is the rationale of *this* creation. Let us be satisfied with our universe, let us make the best use possible of our life upon earth and the rest will come in its time.

It is purposely, mind you, that I have not mentioned the ego as one of the causes of the sense of individuality. For the ego being a falsehood and an illusion, the sense of individuality would itself be false and illusionary (as Buddha and Shankara affirm), whereas the origin of individualisation being in the Supreme Himself, the ego is only a passing deformation, necessary for the moment, which will disappear when its utility is over, when the Truth-Consciousness will be established. (4-173,174)

Transformation of the Ego

Do you have photographs of the time you were very young? And the photographs when you were ten, twenty, thirty years old—it is because one very much wants to do so that one recognises oneself; otherwise, truly, one is not at all the same. . . . When you were this height and now when you are this height, that makes a considerable difference! So, there we are . . .

All this . . . it is not in order to swamp you that I tell you all this. It is only in order to tell you that before speaking of merging one's ego in the Divine, one must first know a little what one is. The ego is there. Its necessity is that you become conscious, independent beings, individualised—I mean in the sense of independent—that you may not be the public square where everything goes criss-cross! That you may exist in yourselves. That is why there is an ego. It is like that; that is why also there is a skin, like that . . . though truly, even physical forces pass through the skin. There is vibration which goes a certain distance. But still, it's the skin that prevents us from blending into one another. But everything else must be like that too.

And then, later, one offers all this to the Divine. Years of work are needed. You must not only . . . become conscious of yourself, conscious in all details, but you must organise what you call "yourself" around the psychic centre, the divine centre of your being, so that it would make a single, coherent, full conscious being. And as this divine centre is itself already consecrated (*Mother makes a gesture of offering*) entirely to the Divine, if everything is organised harmoniously around it, everything is consecrated to the Divine. And so, when the Divine thinks it proper, when the time has come, when the work of individualisation is complete, then the Divine gives you permission to let your ego merge in Him, to live henceforward only for the Divine.

But it is the Divine who takes this decision. You must first have done all this work, become a conscious being, solely and exclusively centred around the Divine and governed by Him. And after all that, there is still an ego; because it is the ego which serves to make you an individual. But once this work is perfect, fully accomplished, then, at that moment, you may tell the Divine, "Here I am, I am ready. Do you want me?" And the Divine usually says, "Yes." All is over, everthing is accomplished. And you become a real instrument for the Divine's work. But first the instrument must be constructed. (6-260,261)

Dissolving the Ego

Yes, that's just what I mean. . . . How can one dissolve, you mean dissolve in the Divine, and lose one's ego?

First of all, one must will it. And then one must aspire with great perseverence, and each time the ego shows itself, one must give it a little rap on the nose (*Mother taps her nose*) until it has received so many raps that it is tired of them and gives up the game.

But usually, instead of rapping it on the nose, one justifies its presence. Almost constantly, when it shows itself, one says, "After all, it is right." And mostly one doesn't even know that it is the ego, one thinks it is oneself. But the first condition is to find it essential not to have the ego any longer. One must really understand that one doesn't want it. It is not so easy. It is not so easy! For one can very well turn words over in the head and say, "I don't want the ego any more, I no longer want to be separated from the Divine." All this goes on inside, like that. But it remains just there, it hasn't much effect on your life. The next moment you do something purely egoistic, you see, and find it quite natural. It doesn't even shock you.

One must first begin to understand truly what this means. The first method . . . you see, there are many stages . . . first, one must try not to be selfish—which is something quite different, isn't it? . . . If you take the English words you understand the difference. In English, you see, there is the word "selfish", and there is also the word "egoism". The ego—"ego"—exists in English, and "selfish". And these are two very different things; in French there is not this distinction. They say, "I don't want to be selfish", you see. But this is a very small thing, very small! People, when they stop being selfish, think they have made tremendous progress! But it's a very small thing. It is simply, oh, it is simply to have a sense of its ridiculousness. You can't imagine how ridiculous these selfish people are!

When one sees them thinking all the time about themselves, referring everything to themselves, governed simply by their own little person, placing themselves in the centre of the universe and trying to organise the whole universe including God around themselves, as though they were the most important thing in the universe. If one could only see oneself objectively, you know, as one sees oneself in a mirror, observe oneself living, it is so grotesque! (*Laughing*) That's enough for you to . . . One suddenly feels that he is becoming—oh, so absolutely ridiculous!

I remember I read in French—it was a translation—a sentence of Tagore's which amused me very much. He was speaking of a little dog. He said . . . he compared it with something . . . I don't remember the details now, but what struck me was this: the little dog was sitting on its mistress's lap and fancying itself the centre of the universe! This struck me very strongly. It is true! I used to know a little dog like this! But there are many like that, almost all are like that. You see, they want everybody to pay attention to them, and in fact they succeed very well. Because when there is a little dog, as when there is a little child—it's almost the same thing—everyone attends to them.

Haven't you noticed that when a child of this height (*Mother indicates the height*) comes along, everything stops? Before that, people could speak, say interesting things, be busy with something higher; but as soon as a child comes along, everybody begins to smile, to mimic a baby, to try to make it speak, to attend to it. One can't bring along a child without everybody fussing over it, wanting to take it, to make it speak. So naturally the child feels itself the centre of the universe! It is quite natural! . . . For a puppy it is the same thing, for a kitten it is the same. It is a kind of . . . it is very poor deformation of a kind of need to protect something that's smaller than oneself. And this is one of the forms, one of the earliest forms of unegoistic manifestation of the ego! It feels so comfortable when it can protect something, busy itself with something much smaller, much weaker than itself, which is almost at its mercy, almost—even entirely—at its mercy, which has no power to resist. And so one feels good and generous because one doesn't crush it!

This is the first manifestation of generosity in the world. But all this, when one can see behind it and a little above, it cures you from being selfish, for truly it is ridiculous! It is truly ridiculous!

So there is a long, long, long way to go before merging one's ego in the Divine.

Merge one's ego in the Divine! But first, one can't merge one's ego in the Divine before becoming completely individualised. Do you know what it means to be *completely* individualised? Capable of resisting all outer influences? Some days ago I received a letter from someone who told me that he was very hesitant about reading books of ordinary literature, for example, novels or dramas, because his nature had an almost insuperable tendency to receive imprints of the characters in these books and to begin living the feelings and thoughts of these characters, the nature of these persons. There are many more people than one would think who are like that. They read a book and while they are reading it they feel within themselves all kinds of emotions, thoughts desires, intentions, plans, even ideals. They are simply just absorbed in the reading of the book. They are not even aware of it, because at least ninety-nine parts of an individual's character are made of soft butter—inedible of course . . . but on which if one presses one's thumb, an imprint is made.

Now, everything is "thumb": an expressed thought, a sentence read, an object looked at, an observation of what someone else does, and of one's neighbor's will. And all these wills . . . you know, when one sees them they are all there, like this, intermingled (*Mother intercrosses her fingers*), each one trying to get the uppermost and causing a kind of perpetual conflict within, outside. . . . It goes in and out of people like that, you see, like electric currents. One is not at all aware of all this, and it is a perpetual conflict of all the wills which they are trying to express themselves; and the strongest one will succeed. But as there are many of these and as one has to fight alone against a great number, it is not easy.

So one is tossed like a cork on the waves of the sea. . . . One day one wants this, the next day one wants that, at one moment one is pushed from this side, at another from that, now one lifts one's face to the sky (*Mother makes the movement*), now one is sunk deep in a hole. And so this is the existence one had!

First one must become a conscious, well-knit *individualised* being, who exists in himself, by himself, independently of all his surroundings, who can hear anything, read anything, see anything without changing. He receives from outside only what he wants to receive; he automatically refuses all that is not in conformity with his plan and nothing can leave an imprint on him unless he agrees to receive the imprint. Then one begins to become an individuality! When one is an individuality, one can make an offering of it.

For unless one possesses something, one cannot give it. First, one must be, and then afterwards one can give oneself.

So long as one does not exist, one can give nothing. And for the separative ego to disappear, as you say, one must be able to give oneself entirely, totally without reservation. And to be able to give oneself, one must first exist. And to exist one must be individualised.

If your body were not made in the rigid form it is—for it is terribly rigid, isn't it?—well, if all that were not so fixed, if you had no skin, here, like this, solid, if externally you were the reflection of what you are in the vital and mental fields, it would be worse than being a jelly-fish! Everything would fuse into everything else, like this. . . . Oh, what a mess it would be! That is why it was at first necessary to give a very rigid form. Afterwards we complain about it. We say, "The physical is fixed, it is a nuisance; it lacks plasticity, it lacks suppleness, it hasn't that fluidity which can enable us to merge into the Divine." But this was absolutely necessary, for without this . . . if you simply went out of your body (most of you can't do it because the vital being is hardly more individualised than the physical), if you came out of your body and went into the vital world, you would see that all things there intermingle, they are mixed, they divide; all kinds of vibrations, currents of forces come and go, struggle, try to destroy one another, take possession of each other, absorb each other, throw each other out . . . and so it goes on! But it is very difficult to find a real personality in all this. These are forces, movements, desires, vibrations.

There are individualities, there are personalities! But these are powers. People who are individualised in that world are either heroes or devils!

And now, in the mind . . . If only you become conscious of your physical mind in itself . . . Some people have called it a public square, because everything comes there, goes across, passes, comes back. . . . All ideas go there, they enter at one place, leave by another, some are here, some there, and it is a public square, not very well organised, for usually ideas meet and knock into one another, there are accidents of all kinds. But then one becomes aware: "*What can I call my mind?*" or "*What is my mind?*"

One needs years of very attentive, very careful, very reasonable, very coherent work, organisation, selection, construction, in order to succeed simply in forming, oh, simply this little thing, *one's own way of thinking!*

One believes he has his own way of thinking. Not at all. It depends totally upon the people one speaks with or the books he has read or on the mood he is in. It depends also on whether you have a good or bad digestion, it depends on whether you are shut up in a room without proper ventilation or whether you are in the open air; it depends on whether you have a beautiful landscape before you; it depends on whether there is sunshine or rain! You are not aware of it, but you think all kinds of things, completely different according to a heap of things which have nothing to do with you!

And for this to become coordinated, coherent, logical thought, a long thorough work is necessary. And then, the best of the business is that when you have succeeded in making a beautiful, well-formed, very strong, very powerful mental construction, the first thing you will be told is, "You must break this so that you can unite with the Divine!" But so long as you haven't made it, you cannot unite with the Divine because you have nothing to give to the Divine except a mass of things which are not yourself! *One must first exist in order to be able to give oneself.* I am repeating what I said a while ago.

Truly, in the present state of the world, the only thing one can give the Divine is one's body. But that's what one doesn't give Him. Yes, one can try to consecrate one's work! But still, here there are so many elements which are not true!

You want to merge your body in the Divine, eh? Just try! How are you going to do this? You can merge your mind, you can merge your vital, you can fuse all your emotions, you can fuse all your aspirations, you can fuse all that, but your body—how are you going to do that? You are not going to melt it in a boiling-pot! (*Laughter*) And yet it is the only thing about which you can say with certitude, "It is", and give a name to it; yet even your name is a convention . . . but still, you are in the habit of calling yourself by a certain name—say, "This, this is I." You look at yourself in a mirror, and although what you were twenty years ago is very different from what you are now . . . it is unrecognisable . . . still something makes you say all the same, "yes, this is I." Yes? "I am so-and-so"—Peter, Louis, Jack, Andre, whoever it may be. . . . (6-254,255,256,257,258,259)

The Shadow

For that, first of all, you must become conscious of it, you see, put it right in front of you, and cut the links which attach to it to your consciousness. It is a work of inner psychology, you know.

One can see, when one studies oneself very attentively. . . . For example, if you observe yourself, you see that one day you are very generous. Let us take this, it is easy to understand. Very generous: generous in your feelings, generous in your sensations, generous in your thoughts and even in material things; that is, you understand the faults of others, their intentions, weaknesses, even nasty movements. You see all this, and you are full of good feelings, of generosity. You tell yourself, "Well . . . everyone does the best he can!"—like that.

Another day—or perhaps the very next minute—you will notice in yourself a kind of dryness, fixity, something that is bitter, that judges severely, that goes as far as bearing a grudge, has rancour, would like the evil-doer punished, that almost has feelings of vengeance; just the very opposite of former! One day someone harms you and you say, "Doesn't matter! He did not know" . . . or "He couldn't do otherwise". . . or "That's his nature" . . . or "He could not understand!" The next day—or perhaps an hour later—you say, "He must be punished! He must pay for it! He must be made to feel that he has done wrong!"—with a kind of rage; and you want to take things, you want to keep them for yourself, you have all the feelings of jealousy, envy, narrowness, you see, just the very opposite of the other feeling.

This is the dark side. And so, the moment one sees it, if one looks at it and doesn't say, "It is I", if one says, "No, it is my shadow, it is the being I must throw out of myself", one puts on it the light of the other part, one tries to bring them face to face; and with the knowledge and light of the other, one doesn't try so much to convince—because that is very difficult—but one compels it to remain quiet . . . first to stand farther away, the one flings it very far away so that it can no longer return—putting a great light on it. There are instances in which it is possible to change, but this is very rare. There are instances in which one can put upon this being—or his shadow—put upon it such an intense light that it transforms it, and it changes into what is the truth of your being.

But this is a rare thing. . . . It can be done, but it is rare. Usually, the best thing is to say, "No, this is not I! I don't want it! I have nothing to do with this movement, it doesn't exist for me, it is something contrary to my nature!" And so, by dint of insisting and driving it away, finally one separates oneself from it.

But one must first be clear and sincere enough to see the conflict within oneself. Usually one doesn't pay any attention to these things. One goes from one extreme to the other. You see, you can say, to put it in very simple words: one day I am good, the next day I am bad. And this seems quite natural. . . . Or even, sometimes for one hour you are good and the next hour you are wicked; or else, sometimes the whole day through one is good and suddenly one becomes wicked, for a minute very wicked, all the more wicked as one was good! Only, one doesn't observe it, thoughts cross one's mind, violent, bad, hateful things, like that . . . Usually one pays no attention to it. But this is what must be caught! As soon as it manifests, you must catch it like this (*Mother makes a movement*) with a very firm grip, and then hold it, hold it up to the light and say, "No! I don't want you! I—don't—want—you! I have nothing to do with this! You are going to get out of here, and you won't return!"

And this is something—an experience that one can have daily, or almost . . . when one has those movements of great enthusiasm, great aspiration, when one suddenly becomes conscious of the divine goal, the urge towards the Divine, the desire to take part in the divine work, when one comes out of oneself in a great joy and great force . . . and then, a few hours later, one is miserable for a tiny little thing; one indulges in so petty, so narrow, so commonplace of self-interestedness, has such a dull desire . . . and all the rest has evaporated as if it did not exist. One is quite accustomed to contradictions; one doesn't pay attention to this and that is why all these things live comfortably together as neighbours. One must first discover them and prevent them from intermingling in one's consciousness: decide between them, separate the shadow from the light. Later one can get rid of the shadow. (6-262,263,264)

The Evil Persona

You have said: "Everyone possess . . . two opposite tendencies of character, . . . which are like the light and the shadow of the same thing."[1]

Why are things made in this way? Can't one have only the light?

". . . Everyone possesses in a large measure, and the exceptional individual in an increasing degree of precision, two opposite tendencies of character, in almost equal proportions, which are like the light and the shadow of the same thing. Thus someone who has the capacity of being exceptionally generous will suddenly find an obstinate avarice rising up in his nature, the courageous man will be a coward in some part of his being and the good man will suddenly have wicked impulses. In this way life seems to endow everyone not only with the possibility of expressing an ideal, but also with contrary elements representing in a concrete manner the battle he has to wage and the victory he has to win for the realisation to become possible. Consequently, all life is an education pursued more or less consciously, more or less willingly."

Yes, if one eliminates the shadow. But it must be eliminated. That does not happen by itself. The world as it is is a mixed world. You cannot have an object which gets the light from one side without its casting a shadow on the other. It is like that, and indeed it is the shadows which make you see the lights. The world is like that, and to have only the light one must definitely go through the entire discipline necessary for eliminating the shadow. This is what I have explained a littler farther; I have said that this shadow was like a sign of what you had to conquer in your nature in order to be able to realise what you have come to do. If you have a part to play, a mission to fulfill, you will always carry in yourself the main difficulty preventing you from realising it, so that you have within your reach the victory you must win. If you had to fight against a difficulty which is everywhere on earth, it would be very difficult (you would need to have a very vast consciousness and a very great power), while if you carry in your own nature just the shadow or defect you must conquer, well, it is there, within your reach: you see all the time the effects of this thing and can fight it directly, immediately. It is a very practical organization.

You haven't seen in the *Bulletin* that letter of Sri Aurobindo's: The "Evil Persona"? It is in the *Bulletin*. The thing is very well explained there.[1] (6-16,17)

Note to Chapter 2

[1] The "Evil Persona": "What you say about the "Evil Persona" interests me greatly as it answers to my consistent experience that a

person great endowed for the work has, always or almost always,—perhaps one ought not to make a too rigid universal rule about these things—a being attached to him, sometimes appearing like a part of him, which is just the contradiction of the thing he centrally represents in the work to be done. Or, if it is not there at first, not bound to his personality, a force of this kind enters into his environment as soon as he begins his movement to realise. Its business seems to be to oppose, to create stumblings and wrong conditions, in a word, to set before him the whole problem of the work he has started to do. It would seem as if the problem could not, in the occult economy of things, be solved otherwise than by the predestined instrument making the difficulty his own. That, would explain many things that seem very disconcerting on the surface."

(Letters on Yoga, Cent. Vol. 24, p. 1660)

(6-16,17)

3

IDENTIFICATION

Our educational system primarily teaches us to learn about something or someone by study and observation, i.e., we process information. But this method is unsatisfactory when we inquire into our own true identity, our personal relationships, nature, the Divine Will and Divine Love. We find that knowing is the experience resulting from the merging of subject and object. We know because we become the object of our knowing and we feel what the object is experiencing. It could be said that we can only truly know through identification in consciousness.

Identification in Relationships

If one succeeds in identifying himself with something, well, one becomes this thing for a time, and becoming this thing one knows all that is in it, without needing either to guess or to construct. That's all.

Of course, there is also a form of foresight, but this does not have altogether the same nature. Foresight usually comes from the faculty of knowing by identity. If one can project his consciousness into something—a circumstance or an event or a person—if one can project his consciousness, well, one receives, afterwards, the precise indication of the thing with which the consciousness was mingled. And this leads gradually to a total and absolute knowledge. In fact it is the only way of knowing, and if one pushes this far enough and succeeds in identifying himself with the Divine, one has the divine knowledge, and this is not impossible. It is something possible because the universe is made like that, for that. Only, it has gone off the right track; for what reasons, one doesn't know. Ah, what strange things we see! . . . To be sure that one knows, and then, at the same time to wonder how it happens.

You have never tried to enter another person's consciousness to know exactly what is going on there? Not projecting your consciousness into someone else, because then you find yourself inside him and this is not interesting—but entering into relation with his consciousness which is within him, for example when, for one reason or another, you don't see things eye to eye; one sees them in one way, the other in another. If people are reasonable they do not quarrel. But if they are not reasonable, they begin quarrelling. Then, instead of quarrelling, the best thing to do is to enter into the other's consciousness and ask yourself why he says things like that, what is it that pushes him to do this or say that? What is the inner reason, what is his vision of things which makes him take this attitude? It is extremely interesting. If you do this, immediately you stop being angry. First thing: you can no longer be angry. So this is already a great gain. But also, if the other continues being angry, it has no effect on you.

And then, later, one can try to identify oneself more perfectly and prevent the movements of division and deformation and stop quarrels. Very useful. (6-424,425)

Knowledge by Identification

Yes, there is a way: it is by identification. But obviously it is a means which eludes absolutely all physical methods. I think that this weakness comes solely from the method used, because one has remained in an absolutely superficial consciousness; and the phenomenon which took place the first time takes place again a second time. If you push your investigation far enough, you suddenly come to a point where your physical methods are no longer of any worth. And in fact one can know only what one is. So if you want to know the universe, you must become the universe. You cannot become the universe physically, you know; but perhaps there is a way of becoming the universe: it is in the consciousness.

If you identify your consciousness with the universal consciousness, then you know what is happening.

But that's the only way; there are no others. It is an absolute fact that one knows only what one is, and if one wants to know something, one must become that. So you see, there are many people who say, "It is impossible", but that's because they remain on a certain plane. It is obvious that if you remain only on the material plane or even on the mental plane, you cannot. . . . (7-319)

Methods of Identification

How do you know the character of a man by looking at his eyes?

Not only by looking at his eyes. I know the character of a man through self-identification. And then outwardly, if you want, the eyes are like doors or windows: there are some which are open, so one enters within, goes very deep inside, and one may see everything that happens there. There are others which are partly open, partly closed; others still have a veil, a kind of curtain; and then there are others which are fastened, locked up, doors closed so well that they cannot be opened. Indeed, this is already an indication, it gives an indication of the strength of the inner life, the sincerity and transparency of the being. And so, through these doors that are open I enter and identify myself with the person within. And I see what he sees, understand what he understands, think what he thinks, and I could do what he does (but usually I refrain from that!) and in this way I get to know what people are like. And it doesn't need much time; it goes very fast. It can even be done through a photograph, but not so well. A photograph captures only a moment, a minute of somebody; if there were many photographs . . . But still, even with a photograph, by going a little deeper one can have a fairly clear idea. But *all* knowledge is knowledge by identification. That is, one must become that which one wants to know. One may surmise, imagine, deduce, one may reason, but one does not know.

So it is something difficult for human beings?

No, why?

One can learn how to identify oneself. One must learn. It is indispensable if one wants to get out of one's ego. For so long as one is shut up in one's ego, one can't make any progress.

How can it be done?

There are many processes. I'll tell you one.

When I was in Paris, I used to go to many places where there were gatherings of all kinds, people making all sorts of researches, spiritual (so-called spiritual), occult researches, etc. And once I was invited to meet a young lady (I believe she was Swedish) who had found a process of knowledge, exactly a process for learning. And so she explained it to us. We were three or four (her French was not very good but she was quite sure of herself!); she said: "It's like this, you take an object or make a sign on a blackboard or take a drawing—that is not important—take whatever is most convenient for you. Suppose, for instance, that I draw for you . . . (she had a blackboard) I draw a design." She drew a kind of half-geometric design. "Now, you sit in front of the design and concentrate all your attention upon it—upon that design which is there. You concentrate, concentrate without letting anything else enter your consciousness—except that. Your eyes are fixed on the drawing and don't move at all. You are as it were hypnotised by the drawing. You look (and so she sat there, looking), you look, look, look. . . . I don't know, it takes more or less time, but still for one who is used to it, it goes pretty fast. You look, look, look, you *become* that drawing you are looking at. Nothing else exists in the world any longer except the drawing, and then, suddenly, you pass to the other side; and when you pass to the other side you enter a new consciousness, and you know."

We had a good laugh, for it was amusing. But it is quite true, it is an excellent method to practise. Naturally, instead of taking a drawing or any object, you may take, for instance, an idea, a few words. You have a problem preoccupying you, you don't know the solution of the problem; well, you objectify your problem in your mind, put it in the most precise, exact, succinct terms possible, and then concentrate, make an effort; you concentrate only on the words, and if possible on the idea they represent, that is, upon your problem—you concentrate, concentrate, concentrate until nothing else exists but that. And it is true that, all of a sudden, you have the feeling of something opening, and one is on the other side. The other side of what? . . . It means that you have opened a door of your consciousness, and instantaneously you have the solution of your problem.

It is an excellent method of learning "how" to identify oneself.

For instance, you are with someone. This person tells you something, you tell him the contrary (as it usually happens, simply through a spirit of contradiction) and you begin arguing. Naturally, you will never come to any point, except a quarrel if you are ill-natured. But instead of doing that, instead of remaining in your own ideas or your own words, if you tell yourself: "Wait a little, I am going to try and see why he said that to me. Yes, why did he tell me that?" And you concentrate: "Why, why, why?" You stand there, just like that, trying. The other person continues speaking, doesn't he?—and he is very happy too, for you don't contradict him any longer! He talks profusely and is sure he has convinced you. Then you concentrate more and more on what he is saying, and with the feeling that gradually, through his words, you are entering his mind. When you enter his head, suddenly you enter into his way of thinking, and next, just imagine, you understand why he is speaking to you thus! And then, if you have a fairly swift intelligence and put what you have just come to understand alongside what you had known before, you have the two ways together, and so can find the truth reconciling both. And here you have truly made progress. And this is the best way of widening one's thought.

If you are beginning an argument, keep quiet immediately, instantaneously. You must be silent, say nothing at all, and then try to see the thing as the other person sees it—that won't make you forget your own way of seeing it, not at all! but you will be able to put both of them together. And you will truly have made progress, a real progress.

It is the same for everything. In all that you do together with others, if you do not agree, take it as a divine Grace, a marvellous opportunity given you to make a progress. And it is simple: instead of being on this side, you are on the other; instead of looking at yourself, you enter the other person and look. You must have just a little bit of imagination, a little more control over your thoughts, over your movements. But that is not very difficult. When you have tried it out a little, after a while you find it very easy.

You must not just look and then make a mental effort, telling yourself: "Why is it like this and like that? Why does he do that? Why does he say that?" You will never arrive at anything. You won't understand, you will imagine all kinds of explanations which will be worthless and teach you nothing at all except to tell yourself: "That person is stupid or else wicked"—things that lead nowhere. On the other hand, if you only make that little movement, and instead of looking at him as an object quite alien to you, you try to enter within, you enter within, into that little head that's before you, and then, suddenly, you find yourself on the other side, you look at yourself and understand quite well what he is saying—everything is clear, the why, the how, the reason, the feeling which is behind the whole thing. . . . It is an experiment you have the opportunity of making a hundred times a day.

At first you won't succeed very well, but if you persist, you will end up by succeeding admirably. This adds a lot of interest to life. And besides it is a work which really makes you progress, for it makes you come out of that little armour of yours in which you are nicely shut up, in which you knock against everything. You have seen moths knocking against the light, haven't you? . . . Everyone's consciousness is like that, it goes along knocking here, knocking there, for these are things foreign to it. But instead of knocking about, one enters within, then it begins to become a part of oneself. One widens oneself, breathes freely, has enough space to move in, one doesn't knock against anything, one enters, penetrates, understands. And one lives in many places at the same time. It is very interesting, one does it automatically.

For instance, when you are reading a book that interests you very much, a wonderful novel full of exciting adventures, when you are completely absorbed in the story, at times you forget your class-hour or even dinner-time or your bed-time. You are completely absorbed in what you are reading. Well, this is a phenomenon of self-identification. And if you do it with a certain perfection, you succeed in understanding ahead what is going to happen. There is a moment when, being fully absorbed in the story, you come to know (without trying to look for it) towards what end the author is leading you, how he is going to unfold his story and come to his conclusion. For you have identified yourself with the creative thought of the author. You do it more or less perfectly, without knowing that you are doing it, but these are phenomena of self-identification.

There are, in Paris, theatres of the third or fourth rank where sensational dramas are performed. These are suburban theatres. They are not for intellectuals but for the masses, and all the elements are always extremely dramatic, moving. Well, those who go there are mostly very simple people and forget completely that they are in a theatre. They identify themselves with the drama. And so, things like this happen: on the stage there is the traitor hiding behind the door, and the hero comes along, not aware naturally that the traitor is hiding there and he is going to be killed. Now, there are people sitting up there (in what is called the gallery), right up in the theatre, who shout: "Look out, he is there!" (*Laughter*) It has not happened just once, it happens hundreds of times, spontaneously. I had seen a play of this kind called *Le Bossu*, I believe; anyway it was quite a sensational drama and it was being played at the *Théâtre de la Porte Saint-Martin*. In this play there was a room. On the stage a large room could be seen and at its side a small room and . . . I don't remember the story now, but in the small room there was a button which could be pressed, and by pressing the button the ceiling of the bigger room could be brought down on those who were there so as to crush them inexorably! . . . And a warning had been given, people had already spoken about it, passed on the word. And now there was a traitor who had hidden himself in the little room and he knew the trick of the button, and then there was the hero who came in with other people, and they started arguing; and everyone knew that the ceiling was going to come down. . . . I didn't say anything, I remembered I was in the theatre, I was waiting to see how the author was going to get out of this situation to save his hero (for it was evident he couldn't kill him off like that before everybody!). But the others were not at all in the same state. Well, there were spectators who shouted, really shouted: "Look out, mind the ceiling!" That's how it was.

These are phenomena of self-identification. Only, they are involuntary. And this is also one of the methods used today to cure nervous diseases. When someone cannot sleep, cannot be restful because he is too excited and nervous and his nerves are ill and weakened by excessive agitation, he is told to sit in front of an aquarium, for instance—an aquarium, that's very lovely, isn't it?—before an aquarium with pretty little fish in it, goldfish; just to sit there, settle down in an easy-chair and try not to think of anything (particularly not of his troubles) and look at the fish. So he looks at the fish, moving around, coming and going, swimming, gliding, turning, meeting, crossing, chasing one another indefinitely, and also the water flowing slowly and the passing fish. After a while he lives the life of fishes: he comes and goes, swims, glides, plays. And at the end of the hour his nerves are in a perfect state and he is completely restful!

But the condition is that one must not think of one's troubles, simply watch the fish.

Can the Divine be attained in this way?

Do you understand, the only way of knowing the Divine is by identifying oneself with Him. There is no other, there is only one, one single way. Hence, once you are master of this method of identification, you can identify yourself. So you choose your object for identification, you want to identify yourself with the Divine. But so long as you do not know how to identify yourself, a hundred and one things will always come across your path, pulling you here, pulling you there, scattering you, and you will not be able to identify yourself with Him. But if you have learnt how to identify yourself, then you have only to orientate the identification, place it where you want it, and then hold on there until you get a result. It will come very fast if you are master of your power of identification. Yes, it will come very quickly. Ramakrishna used to say that the time could vary between three days, three hours and three minutes. Three days for very slow people, three hours for those who were a little swifter, three minutes for those who are used to it.

Three days for very slow people?

For very slow people, yes. He was asked: "How long does it take one to get identified with the Divine?" that was his answer.

And that means three days without doing anything?

No, not without doing anything. It is not necessary to do nothing simply in order to be identified with the Divine. Evidently you cannot remain seated motionless for three days without doing anything; it would mean you had already attained an extraordinary degree of perfection if you could do that—forget all your needs and remain motionless for three days. No, it is not that he means; the thought must be concentrated solely on the Divine. And he did it before that person, to show him, prove to him that what he was saying was true. That did not take him more than three minutes.

But it is just that, what hinders the experience is the absence of the practice of concentration, and also the absence of one-pointedness, singleness of purpose, of will. One "wants" it for a minute, two minutes, ten minutes, a quarter of an hour, an hour, and afterwards, one wants many other things. . . . One "thinks" about it for a few seconds, and after that thinks of a thousand other things. So naturally in this way you could take an eternity. For indeed, in this you cannot add up; if it could be accumulated like grains of sand, if with every thought you give to the Divine you deposit a little grain of sand somewhere after a time this would make a mountain. But it is not like that, it does not remain. It has no result. It does not accumulate, you cannot go on adding, cannot progress quantitatively—you can progress in intensity, progress qualitatively. Yes, you can learn within yourself how to do it; but what you have done counts only in this way. It does not get accumulated like grains of sand on a dune. Else it would be enough to become quite clever and tell yourself: "Well, I shall give at least a dozen thoughts to the Divine every day." And then, by little bits like that, after some time one has a little hill. . . . (5-219,220,221,222,223,224,225,226)

Self Inquiry to One's True Identity

If you have the philosophic mind, you will ask yourself: "What do I call myself'? Is it my body?—it changes all the time, it is never the same. Is it my feelings?—they change so often. Is it my thoughts?—they are built and destroyed continuously. That is not myself. Where is the self? What is it that gives me this sense of continuity?" If you continue sincerely, you go back a few years. The problem becomes more and more perplexing. You continue to observe, you tell yourself: "It is my memory." But even if one loses one's memory, one would be oneself. If one sincerely continues this profound search, there comes a moment when everything disappears and one single thing exists, that is the Divine, the divine Presence. Everything disappears, dissolves, everything melts away like butter in the sunlight. . . . When one has made this discovery, one becomes aware that one was nothing but a bundle of habits. It is always that which does not know the Divine and is not conscious of the Divine which speaks. In everyone there are these hundreds and hundreds of "selves" who speak and in hundreds of completely different ways—"selves" unconscious, changing, fluid. The self which speaks today is not the same as yesterday's; and if you look further, the self has disappeared. There is only one who remains. That is the Divine. It is the only one that may be seen always the same. And unless you have gone so far . . . (5-17)

Identify with Your Work

Of course, there are other roads. One may simply not try to perfect oneself. One may try to forget oneself in an ever more absorbing work, that is, do what one does as a consecration to the Divine, altogether disinterestedly, but with a plenitude, a self-giving, a total self-forgetfulness: no longer thinking about oneself but about what one is doing. You know this, I have already told you this: if you want to do something well, whatever it may be, any kind of work, the least thing, play a game, write a book, do painting or music or run a race, anything at all, if you want to do it well, you must *become* what you are doing and not remain a small person looking at himself doing it; for if one looks at oneself acting, one is . . . one is still in complicity with the ego. If, in oneself, one succeeds in becoming what one does, it is a great progress. In the least little details, one must learn this. Take a very amusing instance: you want to fill a bottle from another bottle; you concentrate (you may try it as a discipline, as a gymnastic); well, as long as you are the bottle to be filled, the bottle from which one pours, and the movement of pouring, as long as you are only this, all goes well. But it unfortunately you think at a given moment: "Ah! it is getting on well, I am managing well", the next minute it spills over! It is the same for everything, for everything. That is why work is a good means of discipline, for if you want to do the work properly, you must *become* the work instead of being someone who works, otherwise you will never do it well. If your remain "someone who works" and, besides, if your thoughts go vagabonding, then you may be sure that if your are handling fragile things they will break, if you are cooking, you will burn something, or if you are playing a game, you will miss all the balls! It is here, in this, that work is a great discipline. For if truly you want to do it well, this is the only way of doing it.

Take someone who is writing a book, for instance. If he looks at himself writing the book, you can't imagine how dull the book will become; it smells immediately of the small human personality which is there and it loses all its value. When a painter paints a picture, if he observes himself painting the picture, the picture will never be good, it will always be a kind of projection of the painter's personality; it will be without life, without force, without beauty. But if, all of a sudden, he becomes the thing he wants to express, if he becomes the brushes, the painting, the canvas, the subject, the image, the colours, the value, the whole thing, and is entirely inside it and lives it, he will make something magnificent.

For everything, everything, it is the same. There is nothing which cannot be a yogic discipline if one does it properly. And if it is not done properly, even tapasya will be of no use and will lead you nowhere. For it is the same thing, if you do your tapasya, all the time observing yourself doing it and telling yourself, "Am I making any progress, is this going to be better, am I going to succeed?", then it is your ego, you know, which becomes more and more enormous and occupies the whole place, and there is no room for anything else. And we said the other day that the spiritual ego is the worst of all, for it is altogether unconscious of its inferiority, it is convinced it is something very superior, if not absolutely divine!

There we are. When you are at school, you must become the concentration which tries to catch what the teacher is saying, or the thought which enters you or the knowledge you are given. That is what you must be. You must not think of yourself but only of what you want to learn. And you will see that your capacities will immediately be doubled.

What gives most the feeling of inferiority, of limitation, smallness, impotence, is always this turning back upon oneself, this shutting oneself up in the bounds of a microscopic ego. One must widen oneself, open the doors. And the best way is to be able to concentrate upon what one is doing instead of concentrating upon oneself. (4-363,364,365)

Dis-Identify from Troubled Vibrations
Stepping Back

Most of you live on the surface of your being, exposed to the touch of external influences. You live almost projected, as it were, outside your own body, and when you meet some unpleasant being similarly projected you get upset. The whole trouble arises out of your not being accustomed to stepping back. You must always step back into yourself—learn to go deep within—step back and you will be safe. Do not lend yourself to the superficial forces which moved in the outside world. Even if you are in a hurry to do something, step back for a while and you will discover to your surprise how much sooner and with what greater success your work can be done. If someone is angry with you, do not be caught in his vibrations but simply step back and his anger, finding no support or response, will vanish. Always keep your peace, resist all temptations to lose it. Never decide anything without stepping back, never speak a word without stepping back, never throw yourself into action without stepping back. All that belongs to the ordinary world is impermanent and fugitive, so there is nothing in it worth getting upset about. What is lasting, eternal, immortal and infinite—that indeed is worth having, worth conquering, worth possessing. It is Divine Light, Divine Love, Divine Life—it is also Supreme Peace, Perfect Joy and All-Mastery upon earth with the Complete Manifestation as the crowning. When you get the sense of the relativity of things, then whatever happens you can step back and look; you can remain quiet and call on the Divine Force and wait for an answer. Then you will know exactly what to do. Remember, therefore, that you cannot receive the answer before you are very peaceful. Practice that inner peace, make at least a small beginning and go on in your practice until it becomes a habit for you. (3-160)

Knowledge by Unity with the Divine—The Divine Will in the World

Consciousness is the faculty of becoming aware of anything whatsoever through identification with it. But the divine consciousness is not only aware but knows and effects. For, mere awareness is not knowledge. To become aware of a vibration, for instance, does not mean that you know everything about it. Only when the consciousness participates in the divine consciousness does it get full knowledge by identification with the object. Ordinarily, identification leads to ignorance rather than knowledge, for the consciousness is lost in what it becomes and is unable to envisage proper causes, concomitants and consequences. Thus you identify yourself with a movement of anger and your whole being becomes one angry vibration, blind and precipitate, oblivious of everything else. It is only when you stand back, remain detached in the midst of the passionate turmoil that you are able to see the process with a knowing eye. So knowledge in the ordinary state of being is to be obtained rather by stepping back from a phenomenon, to watch it without becoming identified with it. But the divine consciousness identifies itself with its object and knows it thoroughly, because it always becomes one with the essential truth or law inherent in each fact. And it not only knows, but, by knowing, brings about what it wants. To be conscious is for it to be effective—each of its movements being a flash of omnipotence which, besides illumining, blazes its way ultimately to the goal dictated by its truth-nature.

Your ordinary consciousness is very much mixed up with unconsciousness—it fumbles, strains and is thwarted, while by unity with the Supreme you share the Supreme Nature and get the full knowledge whenever you turn to observe any object and identify yourself with it. (3-167)

Identifying with Others

But how can we understand?

Ah! that indeed depends upon you.

The first thing is to learn how to know by identity. That is indispensable when one has the responsibility for others. To learn how to guide other people, the first indispensable step is to know how to enter into their minds so as to know them—not to project one's thought, imagine what they are, but go out of oneself and enter into them, to know what is happening there. Then, in this way, one knows them because one is they. When one knows only oneself in others, that means one knows nothing. One may be completely mistaken. One imagines it is like this or that—one judges by appearances or else through mental preferences, preconceived ideas; that is to say, one knows nothing. But there is one condition in which one doesn't even need to know, to try to know what somebody is like: one can't do otherwise but feel what he is, for he is a projection of oneself. And unless one knows how to do that, one can never do what is necessary for people—unless one feels as they feel, thinks as they think, unless one is able to enter into them as though one were they themselves. That is the only way. If you try to know with a small active mind, you will never know anything—nor by looking at people and telling yourself: "Why, he does this in this way and that way, so he must be like that." That is impossible.

So, the first task of those who have a responsibility—for instance, those who are in charge of educating other children, taking care of others, from rulers to teachers and monitors—their first task is to learn how to identify themselves with the others, to feel as they do. Then one knows what one should do. One keeps one's inner light, keeps one's consciousness where it ought to be, very high above, in the light, and at the same time gets identified, and so one fees what they are, what their reactions are, what their thoughts, and one holds that before the light one has: one succeeds in thinking out perfectly well what should be done for them. You will tell each one what he needs to hear, you will act with each one as is necessary to make him understand. And that is why it is a wonderful grace to have the responsibility for a certain number of people, for that obliges you to make the most essential progress. And I hasten to tell you that ninety-nine times out of a hundred, people don't make it. But that is exactly why things are in such a bad way. Particularly those who have the responsibility of governing a country—this is the last thing they think about! They are very eager rather to keep their way of seeing and their way of feeling, and fiercely refrain from realising the needs of those over whom they rule. But indeed one can see that the results is not up to much; so far it is evident that it can't be said that governments have been remarkable institutions. It is the same thing on all the levels: there are small governments, there are big governments. But the laws are the same, for all. And unless, when giving a lesson, you are able, there and then, to take in the entire atmosphere, to gather the vibrations around people, put them all together, keep all that before you, and become aware of what you can do with this stuff (with the vibrations you can spread, the forces you can give out, those which will be received, those which will be assimilated), unless you do that, mostly you are wasting your time, you too. In order to do the least work, one must make a lot of progress. (5-299,300,301)

Divine Love

How can one become conscious of Divine Love and an instrument of its expression?

First, to become conscious of anything whatever, you must will it. And when I say "will it", I don't mean saying one day, "Oh! I would like it very much", then two days later completely forgetting it.

To will it is a constant, sustained, concentrated aspiration, an almost exclusive occupation of the consciousness. This is the first step. There are many others: a very attentive observation, a very persistent analysis, a very keen discernment of what is pure in the movement and what is not. If you have an imaginative faculty, you may try to imagine and see if your imagination tallies with reality. There are people who believe that it is enough to wake up one day in a particular mood and say, "Ah! how I wish to be conscious of divine Love, how I wish to manifest divine Love. . . ." Note, I don't know how many millions of times one feels within a little quivering of human instinct and imagines that if one had at one's disposal divine Love, great things could be accomplished, and one says, "I am going to try and find divine Love and we shall see the result." This is the worst possible way. Because, before having even touched the very beginning of realisation you have spoilt the result. You must take up your search with a purity of aspiration and surrender which in themselves are already difficult to acquire. You must have worked much on yourself only to be *ready* to aspire to this Love. If you look at yourself very sincerely, very straight, you will see that as soon as you begin to think of Love it is always your little inner tumult which starts whirling. All that aspires in you wants certain vibrations. It is almost impossible, without being far advanced on the yogic path, to separate the vital essence, the vital vibration from your conception of Love. What I say is founded on an assiduous experience of human beings. Well, for you, in the state in which you are, as you are, if you had a contact with pure divine Love, it would seem to you colder than ice, or so far-off, so high that you would not be able to breathe; it would be like the mountain-top where you would feel frozen and find it difficult to breathe, so very far would it be from what you normally feel. Divine Love, if not clothed with a psychic or vital vibration, is difficult for a human being to perceive. One can have an impression of grace, of a grace which is something so far, so high, so pure, so impersonal that . . . yes, one can have the feeling of grace, but it is with difficulty that one feels Love. (4-244,245)

Love in Nature

The movement of love is not limited to human beings and it is perhaps less distorted in other worlds than in the human. Look at the flowers and trees. When the sun sets and all becomes silent, sit down for a moment and put yourself into communion with Nature: you will feel rising from the earth, from below the roots of the trees and mounting upward and coursing through their fibres up to the highest outstretching branches, the aspiration of an intense love and longing,—a longing for something that brings light and gives happiness, for the light that is gone and they wish to have back again. There is a yearning so pure and intense that if you can feel the movement in the trees, your own being too will go up in an ardent prayer for the peace and light and love that are unmanifested here. Once you have come in contact with this large, pure and true Divine love, if you have felt it even for a short time and in its smallest form, you will realise what an abject thing human desire has made of it. It has become in human nature something low, brutal, selfish, violent, ugly, or else it is something weak and sentimental, made up of the pettiest feeling, brittle, superficial, exacting. And this baseness and brutality or this self-regarding weakness they call love! (3-72)

Identification with Pain

For you are always under the illusion that pain belongs to you. This is not true. Pain is something thrust upon you. The same event could occur, *exactly* the same in all its details, without its inflicting the shadow of a pain on you; on the contrary, sometimes it can fill you with ecstatic joy. And it is exactly the same thing. But in some case, you are open to the adverse forces you want to reject from yourself, and in the other you are not, your are already too far away from them to be affected by them any longer; and so, instead of feeling the negative side they represent, you feel only the positive side the Divine represents in the experience. It is the divine Grace which makes you progress, and with the divine Grace you feel the divine Joy. But instead of identifying yourself with the Grace which makes you progress, you identify yourself with the ugly things you want to get rid of; and so, naturally, you feel like it and suffer.

That is an experiment you can make if you are just a little conscious. There is something in you which you don't want, something bad—for one reason or another you don't want it, you want to pull it out—well, if you identify yourself ever so little with that thing, you feel the pain of the extraction; if, on the contrary, you identify yourself with the divine Force which comes to liberate you, you feel the joy of the divine Grace—and you experience the deep delight of the progress you have made.

And this is a sure sign for you, a sure indication what you identify yourself with. If you are identified with the forces from below, you suffer; if you are identified with the forces from above, you are happy. And I am not speaking about feeling pleasure: you must not think that when one jumps about, dances, shouts and plays, one is identified with the divine forces—one may or may not be. That is not what I am speaking of. I am speaking of the divine Joy, the inner Joy which is unalloyed.

Each time a shadow passes, with what may be just an uneasiness or what may become a severe pain or an unbearable suffering, through the whole range, from the smallest to the greatest—as soon as it appears in your being, you may tell yourself, "Ah, the enemy is there!"—in one form or another. (8-84,85)

Love: The Joy of Identity

Sweet Mother, I did not understand this: "At the beginning of this manifestation, in the purity of its origin, love is composed of two movements, two complementary poles of the urge towards complete oneness. On the one hand there is the supreme power of attraction and on the other the irresistible need for absolute self-giving."

There is nothing to understand; it is a fact. You don't know what "the power of attraction" means? You don't know what "the need for self-giving" means? . . . Well, you put them face to face and when they unite, that creates love. It is as simple as that. If you wish, it is like the obverse and reverse of the same medal; but it is not the obverse and reverse. These two things are destined to unite by their very nature and it is through this meeting that love in its external manifestation is born.

After that you have said: "No other movement could have better bridged the abyss that was created when in the individual being consciousness was separated from its origin and became unconsciousness."

Yes, because the moment the individual consciousness broke off from the divine Consciousness, from its divine source, it created the sense of separation. The moment the individual consciousness ceased to follow, did not remain identified with the movement of the divine Consciousness, this produced a separation. The divine Consciousness follows its own movement, and if the individual consciousness does not remain united and does not follow or changes the course or slows down on the way, this creates a separation. And it is this separation that is the cause of all misery. All the miseries in the universe are the result of this separation of the individual consciousness which, for some reason or other, did not remain identified with the primal Consciousness, its origin, and separated from it. Separated . . . it did not deliberately separate itself, but it did not remain identified. So, not remaining identified, while the divine Consciousness followed one particular movement, it followed another, and naturally this caused them to move farther and farther away from each other. Let us take an illustration: one goes forward with a certain movement, a certain speed, and the other, not having remained united, is unable to follow and consequently, little by little, falls farther and farther behind, far, far, very far; the first one goes ahead and the other is left behind. It goes limping along while the first one flies; it takes one step while the other leaps. So this brings about a greater and greater separation. And it is this separation which has created all other separations, and it is all these separations which have caused universal misery—or in any case the misery on earth, the one we know. It began by a separation of consciousness and finished with a separation of worlds and of the elements of matter. It began by a division of consciousness and ended with the kind of division we see (*Mother points at those around her*). There are thousands of things all separated from one another and it is due to this that there are all these miseries. If they had remained united in consciousness, there would have been no misery. But as the consciousness was separated, this separation of consciousness caused the separation of forms and the separation of forms produced all the miseries.

If the sense of unity were re-established, the miseries would disappear.

Before our nature is transformed, can a person love another truly?

Love another? I have said there that it is impossible. I have said that if one wants to know what love is, one must love the Divine. Then there is a chance of knowing what love is. I have said that one grows into the likeness of what one loves. So if one loves the Divine, gradually, through this effort of love, one grows more and more like the Divine, and then one can be identified with the divine love and know what it is, otherwise one can't.

Inevitably, love between two human beings, whatever it may be, is always made of ignorance, lack of understanding, weakness and that terrible sense of separation. It is as though one wanted to enter the presence of a unique Splendour and that the first thing one did was to put a curtain, two curtains, three curtains between oneself and that Splendour, and one is quite surprised to have only a vague impression and not at all the thing itself. The first thing to do is to remove the curtains, to take them all away, to go through and find oneself in the presence of the Splendour. And then you will know what that Splendour is. But if you put veil after veil between it and yourself, you will never see it. You may have a sort of vague feeling like "Oh! there is something", but that is all.

Naturally, there are all those who don't care for the Splendour, who turn their back upon it and live in their instincts, who are just animals, a little perfected. Let us not speak of these. We have only to let them do what they like, that is of no importance at all. They don't affect us. It is not for them that I have written these things.

In order to know how to love truly, should the nature be transformed?

The quality of love is in proportion to the transformation of your consciousness.

I don't understand.

It is childishly simple. If you have the consciousness of an animal, you will love like an animal. If you have the consciousness of an ordinary man, you will love like an ordinary man. If you have the consciousness of an élite being, you will love like an élite being, and if you have god's consciousness, you will love like a god. It is simple! That's what I have said. And so, if by an effort for progress and inner transformation, by aspiration and growth, you pass from one consciousness to the other and your consciousness becomes vaster and vaster, well, the love you experience will be vaster and vaster. That is quite clear!

You take the purest water, water from the crystalline rocks, you collect it in a fairly large vase, and then, in this vase there is a little mud, or much, or a huge quantity of mud. And you could not say it is the same water which came down, yet it is the same, only you have mixed it with so many things in your vase that it no longer resembles it at all! Well, love in its essence is an absolutely pure, crystalline perfect thing. In the human consciousness it gets mixed with a fairly considerable amount of mud. So it becomes more and more muddy in proportion to the amount of mud.

It has been said that the tiger's need for devouring is one of the first expressions of love in the world. I think that long before the tiger, there must have been primitive creatures in the depths of the sea which had only this one function: a stomach. The existed only as stomachs. And so they swallowed—that was their one occupation. Evidently that was one of the first results of the Power of Love infiltrating into Matter, for before this there was nothing: there was perfect inconscience, complete immobility, nothing stirred. With Love movement began: the awakening of consciousness and the movement of transformation. Well, the first forms, it may be said, were the first expression of Love in Matter. So we can go from the need of swallowing which is the only consciousness—a need for swallowing, of uniting—right up to . . . Excuse me, we say that Love is the power of the world—it is a primitive way of uniting with things, but it is a very direct way: one swallows and absorbs the thing; well, the tiger indeed takes a great joy in it. So there is a joy already, it is already quite a high form of love. You may go higher and end up with one of the highest expressions of love in human beings: the total self-giving to what is loved, that is, to die for one's country or to give one's life to defend somebody, and things like that. That indeed is already . . . fairly high. It is still mixed with some mud. It is not the highest form but it is already something. And you see all the steps, don't you? Well, from this one has still to climb a good deal to reach the true expression, to reach what I have described, which is at the summit of the ascent—I would not like to travesty my own words (*Mother takes her copy of* "The Four Austerities" *and reads*):

> *"Love is, in its essence, the joy of identity; it finds its expression in the bliss of union."*

At first, before the emanation of Love, there is something which we may express very clumsily by "the joy of identity". That indeed is very difficult to conceive, for human thought cannot conceive of things except by their opposites, while the supreme phase comes when love has gone the whole round of the universe in order to climb back to its origin; then it has the result of all that experience it gained and it returns to its starting-point. It goes back to its starting-point with something *more* which it did not have before starting: the experience of the universe. And fundamentally, that is the very *raison d'être* of creation. It is because the consciousness would not be what it is if it had not expressed itself in a creation. Well, the return from creation—which, mark it, is not something that takes place in time—is very difficult to conceive, for we conceive time and space and for us things are successive, one thing follows another, but if it were possible to conceive a total movement which would englobe everything and be at once the beginning and the end, and which would contain everything, well, this return, which would not be a return in time, which would be a return in consciousness—how shall I explain that to you?—the return of love to its origin, instead of being simply the joy of identity, becomes the ecstasy of union—and obviously, if one sees from the pure psychological point of view, there is an enriching of consciousness which comes from the experience gained in the universe; that is, there is a richness of content and a plenitude of consciousness which would not be there if there had been no manifested universe. And that obviously is the most logical explanation, the most logical reason for the creation. (6-100,101,102,103,104,105)

4

CONCENTRATION AND MEDITATION

If identification is necessary to gain true knowledge of an object, then concentration and meditation are certainly necessary steps in that process. Concentration is also essential for success in the ordinary life.

In Integral Yoga, meditation takes on a much more dynamic quality for its purpose is transformation of our psyche, not escape. In fact, physical work assumes an equal importance if done with the right attitude, as an offering to the Divine. Meditation can become a 24-hour a day practice, even during sleep, and not simply an isolated event alone in a room somewhere, for one's life must also be transformed.

The Flame of Aspiration

It is very difficult to meditate. There are all kinds of meditations. . . . You may take an idea and follow it to arrive at a given result—this is an active meditation; people who want to solve a problem or to write, meditate in this way without knowing that they are meditating. Others sit down and try to concentrate on something without following an idea—simply to concentrate on a point in order to intensify one's power of concentration; and this brings about what usually happens when you concentrate upon a point: if you succeed in gathering your capacity for concentration sufficiently upon a point whether mental, vital or physical, at a given moment you pass through and enter into another consciousness. Others still try to drive out from their head all movements, ideas, reflexes, reactions and to arrive at a truly silent tranquility. This is extremely difficult; there are people who have tried for twenty-five years and not succeeded, for it is somewhat like taking a bull by the horns.

There is another kind of meditation which consists in

being as quiet as one can be but without trying to stop all thoughts, for there are thoughts which are purely mechanical and if you try to stop these you will need years, and into the bargain you will not be sure of the result; instead of that you gather together all your consciousness and remain as quiet and peaceful as possible, you detach yourself from external things as though they do not interest you at all, and all of a sudden, you brighten the flame of aspiration and throw into it everything that comes to you so that the flame may rise higher and higher, higher and higher; you identify yourself with it and you go up to the extreme point of your consciousness and aspiration, thinking of nothing else—simply, an aspiration which mounts, mounts, mounts, without thinking a minute of the result, of what may happen and specially of what may not, and above all without desiring that something may come—simply, the joy of an aspiration which mounts and mounts and mounts, intensifying itself more and more in a constant concentration. And there I may assure you that what happens is the best that can happen. That is, it is the maximum of your possibilities which is realised when you do this. These possibilities may be very different according to individuals. But then all these worries about trying to be silent, going behind appearances, calling a force which answers, waiting for an answer to your questions, all that vanishes like an unreal vapour. And if you succeed in living consciously in this flame, in this column of mounting aspiration, you will see that even if you do not have an immediate result, after a time something will happen. (4-104,105)

Meditation in Action

> *"Then you have rather to make an effort to stop meditating: it becomes difficult to stop meditation, difficult to stop thinking of the Divine, difficult to come down to the ordinary consciousness."*
>
> *Questions and Answers 1929* (21 April)

How I wish this would become true for everybody!

You may be engaged in the most active action, for example, in playing basketball, which needs a great deal of movement, and yet not lose the attitude of inner meditation and concentration upon the Divine. And when you get that, you will see that all you do changes its quality; not only will you do it better, but you will do it with an altogether unexpected strength, and at the same time keep your consciousness so high and so pure that nothing will be able to touch you any longer. And note that this can go so far that even if an accident occurs, it will not hurt you. Naturally, this is a peak, but it is a peak to which one can aspire.

Do not fall into the very common error of believing that you must sit in an absolutely quiet corner where nobody passes by, where you are in a classical position and altogether immobile, in order to be able to meditate—it is not true. What is needed is to succeed in meditating under all circumstances, and I call "meditating" not emptying your head but concentrating yourself in a contemplation of the Divine; and if you keep this contemplation within you, all that you do will change its quality—not its appearance, for apparently it will be the same thing, but its quality. And life will change its quality, and you, you will feel a little different from what you were, with a peace, a certitude, an inner calm, an unchanging force, something which never gives way.

In that state it will be difficult to do you harm—the forces always try, this world is so full of adverse forces which seek to upset everything . . . but they succeed in a very small measure, only in the measure necessary to force you to make a new progress.

Each time you receive a blow from life, tell yourself immediately, "Ah, I have to make a progress"; then the blow becomes a blessing. Instead of tucking your head between your shoulders, you lift it up with joy and you say, "What is it I have to learn? I want to know. What is it I have to change? I want to know." This is what you should do. (4-121,122)

Imperatives for Meditation

Even if you make yourself an absolute blank, that does not change the nature of your aspiration or alter its domain. In some the aspiration moves on the mental level or in the vital field; some have a spiritual aspiration. On the quality of the aspiration depends the force that answers and the work that it comes to do. To make yourself blank in meditation creates an inner silence; it does not mean that you have become nothing or have become a dead and inert mass. Making yourself an empty vessel, you invite that which shall fill it. It means that you release the stress of your inner consciousness towards realisation. The nature of the consciousness and the degree of its stress determine the forces that you bring into play and whether they shall help and fulfil or fail or even harm and hinder.

There are many varying conditions in which you may meditate and all have their effect upon the forces brought in or brought down and on their working. If you sit alone, it is your own inner and outer condition that matters. If you sit with others, the general condition is of primary importance. But in either case the conditions will always vary and the forces that answer will never be twice the same. A united concentration rightly done can be a great force. There is an old saying that if twelve sincere persons unite their will and their aspiration and call the Divine, the Divine is bound to manifest. But the will must be one- pointed, the aspiration sincere. For those who make the attempt can be united in inertia or even in mistaken or perverse desire, and the result is then likely to be disastrous.

In your meditation the first imperative need is a state of perfect and absolute sincerity in all the consciousness. It is indispensable that you should not deceive yourself or deceive or be deceived by others. Often people have a wish, a mental preference or vital desire; they want the experience to happen in a particular way or to take a turn that satisfies their ideas or desires or preferences; they do not keep themselves blank and unprejudiced and simply and sincerely observe what happens. Then if you do not like what happens, it is easy to deceive yourself; you will see one thing, but give it a little twist and make it something else, or you will distort something simple and straightforward or magnify it into an extraordinary experience. When you sit in meditation you must be as candid and simple as a child, not interfering by your external mind, expecting nothing, insisting on nothing. Once this condition is there, all the rest depends upon the aspiration deep within you. If you ask from within for peace, it will come; if for strength, for power, for knowledge, they too will come, but all in the measure of your capacity to receive it. And if you call upon the Divine, then too—always admitting that the Divine is open to your call, and that means your call is pure enough and strong enough to reach him,—you will have the answer. (3-98,99)

The Process of Meditation

Mother, when you speak we try to understand with the mind, but when you communicate something in silence, on what part of the being should we concentrate?

It is always better, for meditation—you see, we use the word "meditation", but it does not necessarily mean "moving ideas around in the head", quite the contrary—it is always better to try to concentrate in a centre, the centre of aspiration, one might say, the place where the flame of aspiration burns, to gather in all the energies there, at the solar plexus centre and, if possible, to obtain an attentive silence as though one wanted to listen to something extremely subtle, something that demands a complete attention, a complete concentration and total silence. And then not to move at all.

Not to think, not to stir, and make that movement of opening so as to receive all that can be received, but taking good care not to try to know what is happening while it is happening, for if one wants to understand or even to observe actively, it keeps up a sort of cerebral activity which is unfavourable to the fullness of the receptivity—to be silent, as totally silent as possible, in an attentive concentration, and then be still.

If one succeeds in this, then, when everything is over, when one comes out of meditation, some time later—usually not immediately—from within the being something new emerges in the consciousness: a new understanding, a new appreciation of things, a new attitude in life—in short, a new way of being. This may be fugitive, but at that moment, if one observes it, one finds that something has taken one step forward on the path of understanding or transformation. It may be an illumination, an understanding truer or closer to the truth, or a power of transformation which helps you to achieve a psychological progress or a widening of the consciousness or a greater control over your movements, over the activities of the being.

And these results are never immediate. For if one tries to have them at once, one remains in a state of activity which is quite the contrary of true receptivity. One must be as neutral, as immobile, as passive as one can be, with a background of silent aspiration not formulated in words or ideas or even in feelings; something that does this (*gesture like a mounting flame*) in an ardent vibration, but which does not formulate, and above all, does not try to understand.

With a little practice one reaches a state which may be obtained at will, in a few seconds, that is, one doesn't waste any of the meditation time. Naturally, in the beginning, one must slowly quieten the mind, gather up one's consciousness, concentrate; one loses three-quarters of the time in preparing oneself. But when one has practised the thing, in two or three seconds one can get it, and then one benefits from the whole period of receptivity.

Naturally, there are still more advanced and perfected states, but that comes later. But already if one reaches that state, one profits fully by the meditation.

We are going to try. (9-114,115)

Emptiness Vs. Releasing the Stress

In silent meditation, should not one make oneself completely empty? But, then, how can it depend on the one who meditates?

I think there is a confusion between silence in the mind and the complete emptiness in the being, they are two very different things. Besides, I don't see very well how one can make oneself completely empty—one would not exist any longer!

> *"To make yourself blank in meditation creates an inner silence; it does not mean that you have become nothing or have become a dead and inert mass. Making yourself an empty vessel, you invite that which shall fill it. It means that you release the stress of your inner consciousness towards realisation. The nature of the consciousness and the degree of its stress determine the forces that you bring into play and whether they shall help and fulfil or fail or even harm and hinder."*
>
> *Question and Answers 1929* (23 June)

What does "the degree of its stress" mean?

Aspiration and will produce a stress in the being. But I say "degree", for there is also the point upon which the stress works. I say "to make yourself blank" is to release the stress of your consciousness towards realisation, towards the goal you want to realise. The "stress" is the pressure upon a point, what is concentrated upon a point and insists that it be done. Consciousness—the consciousness of the being, individual consciousness—puts a pressure upon a point, you see. We may take the example we were just speaking of: you have a chronic illness, a malformation of the body, a physical defect. Then your consciousness, in its aspiration and will puts a more or less constant stress on the thing it wants to realise, what you want to cure. Well, when you make yourself empty within in meditation (this is one form of meditation if you like), this means that you stop this concentration of will: your consciousness becomes neutral for the moment. Its stress is upon this point (it may be on other points, on things more or less concrete or abstract, but the stress is on one point) and when you make yourself empty you withdraw this pressure, this stress, and you remain like a blank page upon which nothing is written. This is what I call "making yourself empty", not to have any active will concentrated upon one point or another. And so I say the moment you make yourself empty, the stress in effect stops, and yet in your silent aspiration you put yourself in contact with the forces attracted by this stress you usually have, the special point of stress you have normally. That is why I have emphasised the fact that all depends upon the person, because everything depends upon his habitual aspiration, the thing he usually wants to realise, for he is naturally in touch with the forces which will answer his aspiration. So, if for a certain time one stops the activity of this aspiration and remains silently receptive, passive, well, the effect of the habitual aspiration remains and will draw just those forces which ought to answer it. (4-281,282,283)

Individual Vs. Collective Meditation and Prayer

Before the meditation this evening I am going to say a few words to you, because several people have asked me the difference between a collective meditation and an individual meditation.

Individual meditation—I have already explained to you many times the different kinds of meditation that are possible and I won't begin to speak to you about that again.

But collective meditations have been practised in all ages for different reasons, in different ways and with different motives. What may be called a collective meditation is a group of people who gather together for a definite purpose; for example, in all ages it has been a practice to gather for prayers. Naturally in the Churches, it is a sort of collective meditation but even outside the Churches, some people have organised collective meditations for group prayer. These prayers are of two different kinds.

From the beginning of human history, it is known that certain groups of people would meet to express a certain common state of soul: some to sing together the praise of God, hymns, thanksgiving, to express adoration, thankfulness, gratitude, and to praise God; others—and there are historical examples of this—a certain number of people gathered together for a common invocation, for instance, to ask God for something, and this was done all together, united, in the hope that this invocation, this prayer, this asking would carry more weight. There have been some very famous instances. A very old one occurred in 1000 A.D. when some prophets had announced that it was the end of the world and everywhere people gathered together to offer common prayers and ask that the world may not come to an end (!) or anyway, for it to be protected. Much more recently, in modern times, when King George of England was dying of pneumonia, people assembled in England, not only in the churches but even in the streets in front of the royal palace, to offer prayers and ask God to cure him. It so happened that he recovered, and they believed that it was their prayers. . . . That is, of course, the most external form, I could say the most worldly, of group meditation.

In all initiatory groups, in all the spiritual schools of ancient times, group meditation was always practised and in that case the motive was quite different. They assembled for a collective progress, to open together to a force, a light, an influence, and . . . this is more or less what we want to try to do.

However, there are two methods, and this is what I am going to explain to you. In both cases, one must practise as one does in individual meditation, that is, sit in a position at once comfortable enough for one to be able to keep it and yet not too comfortable for one to fall asleep in it! And then you do what I had asked you to do while I used to go for the distribution over there, that is, prepare for the meditation, try to become calm and silent; not only to avoid chattering outwardly, but to try to silence your mind and gather your consciousness which is dispersed in all the thoughts you have and your preoccupations; to gather it, bring it back within yourself as completely as possible and concentrate it here, in the region of the heart, near the solar plexus, so that all the active energies in the head and all that keeps the brain running, may be brought back and concentrated here. This can be done in a few seconds, it can take a few minutes: that depends on each one. Well, this is a preparatory attitude. And then, once this is done—or done as well as you can do it—you may take two attitudes, that is, an active attitude or a passive attitude.

What I call an active attitude is to concentrate on—I shall put it in general terms—on the person who is directing the meditation, with the will to open and receive from him what he intends to give you or the force with which he wants to put you into contact. That is active, for here there is a will at work and an active concentration to open yourself to someone, a concentration on someone.

The other one, the passive one is simply this: to be concentrated as I have told you, then you open yourself as one opens a door; you see, you have a door here (*gesture at the level of the heart*) and once you are concentrated, you open the door and stay like this (*gesture of immobility*). Or else, you may take another image, as if it were a book, and you open your book very wide with its pages completely blank, that is, quite silent, and you stay like that waiting for what is going to happen.

These are the two attitudes. You may take one or the other, according to the day, the occasion, or you may adopt one of them, out of preference, if it helps you more. Both are effective and can have equally good results. (9-37,38,39)

Meditation

"The practice of this Yoga demands a constant inward remembrance of the one central liberating knowledge. . . . In all is the one Self, the one Divine is all; all are in the Divine, all are the Divine and there is nothing else in the universe,—this thought or this faith is the whole background until it becomes the whole substance of the consciousness of the worker. A memory, a self-dynamising meditation of this kind, must and does in its end turn into profound and uninterrupted vision and a vivid and all-embracing consciousness of that which we so powerfully remember or on which we so constantly meditate."

The Synthesis of Yoga, p. 104

Sweet Mother, what does Sri Aurobindo mean by "a self-dynamising meditation"?

It is a meditation that has the power of transforming your being. It is a meditation which makes you progress, as opposed to static meditation which is immobile and relatively inert, and which changes nothing in your consciousness or in your way of being. A dynamic meditation is a meditation of transformation.

Generally, people don't have a dynamic meditation. When they enter into meditation—or at least what they call meditation—they enter into a kind of immobility where nothing stirs, and they come out of it exactly as they went in, without any change either in their being or in their consciousness. And the more motionless it is, the happier they are. They could meditate in this way for eternities, it would never change anything either in the universe or in themselves. That is why Sri Aurobindo speaks of a dynamic meditation which is exactly the very opposite. It is a transforming meditation.

How is it done? Is it done in a different way?

I think it is the aspiration that should be different, the attitude should be different. "Different way"—what do you mean by "way"—(*laughing*) the way of sitting? . . . Not that? The inner way?

Yes.

But for each one it is different.

I think the most important thing is to know why one meditates; this is what gives the quality of the meditation and makes it of one order or another.

You may meditate to open yourself to the divine Force, you may meditate or reject the ordinary consciousness, you may meditate to enter the depths of your being, you may meditate to learn how to give yourself integrally; you may meditate for all kinds of things. You may meditate to enter into peace and calm and silence—this is what people generally do, but without much success. But you may also meditate to receive the Force of transformation, to discover the points to be transformed, to trace out the line of progress. And then you may also meditate for very practical reasons: when you have a difficulty to clear up, a solution to find, when you want help in some action or other. You may meditate for that too.

I think everyone has his own mode of meditation. But if one wants the meditation to be dynamic, one must have an aspiration for progress and the meditation must be done to help and fulfil this aspiration for progress. Then it becomes dynamic. (8-88,89)

Meditation Vs. Concentration

The concentration we have here and the meditation we used to have in the past, are they the same?

No, I told you this the other day, the concentration we have now is the opposite of meditation. In the common meditation we used to have, I tried to unify the consciousness of all who were present and to lift it in an aspiration towards higher regions; it was a movement of ascent, of aspiration—whereas what we do here, in concentration, is a movement of descent. Instead of an aspiration which rises up, what is required is a receptivity which opens so that the Force may enter into you. There are many ways of doing this; each one according to his particular nature should find out the best method. What is asked here is a receptive offering, not of the body or the mind or the vital, of a piece of your being, but of your entire being. No other thing is asked of you, only to *open* yourself; the rest of the work I undertake.

In the meditation there I wanted each one to kindle in himself a flame of aspiration and to rise up as high as possible. Naturally, both are necessary; but the morning meditation, all who had a goodwill could join it at any stage of their development, while here the rule is that only those who really want the perfection of their physical body can come, not those who want to escape from life, escape from themselves, escape from their body to enter into the heights. That is why in the beginning the selection was very strict—it is widening little by ltitle, with profit, I hope. We wanted only those who had truly taken it into their head that they wished to perfect their physical body, who understood that their body had its own value and who sought to perfect it, who wanted to try to make it a receptacle of a higher truth, not an old rag one throws aside saying, "Do not bother me!" On the contrary, to take it up and make of it the best possible instrument, to make it grow, to perfect it as much as it will lend itself to the process. (4-122,123)

Types of Concentration

Concentration is a more active state. You may concentrate mentally, you may concentrate vitally, psychically, physically, and you may concentrate integrally. Concentration or the capacity to gather oneself at one point is more difficult than meditation. You may gather together one portion of your being or consciousness or you may gather together the whole of your consciousness or even fragments of it, that is, the concentration may be partial, total or integral, and in each case the result will be different.

If you have the capacity to concentrate, your meditation will be more interesting and easier. But one can meditate without concentrating. Many follow a chain of ideas in their meditation—it is meditation, not concentration.

Is it possible to distinguish the moment when one attains perfect concentration from the moment when, starting from this concentration, one opens oneself to the universal Energy?

Yes. You concentrate on something or simply you gather yourself together as much as possible for you and when you attain a kind of perfection in concentration, if you can sustain this perfection for a sufficiently long time, then a door opens and you pass beyond the limit of your ordinary consciousness—you enter into a deeper and higher knowledge. Or you go within. Then you may experience a kind of dazzling light, an inner wonder, a beatitude, a complete knowledge, a total silence. There are, of course, many possibilities but the phenomenon is always the same.

To have this experience all depends upon your capacity to maintain your concentration sufficiently long at its highest point of perfection.

To have this experience is it necessary to concentrate every time?

In the beginning, yes, for you have not the capacity to keep what you have acquired, to maintain your concentration at its maximum—you slip back and lose even the memory of the experience you have had. But if you once follow a path, it is easier to follow the same path a second time and so on. The second concentration is therefore easier than the first one. You must persevere in your concentration till you come to the point when you no longer lose the inner contact.

From that time onward you must remain in this inner and higher consciousness from where you can do everything. You see your body and the material world and you know what is to be done and how to do it.

That is the first aim of concentration, but naturally not the last.

To attain that concentration much effort is necessary; an immediate or even a quick result is rarely possible. But if the inner door has once been opened, you may be sure that it will open again if you know how to persevere.

As long as the door has not been opened, you may doubt your capacity, but once opened, no more doubt is possible, if you go on willing and aspiring. (4-8,9)

Meditation on a Sentence

Because that, Mother, becomes a mental function or what?

The sentence is already a mental formation; the mental formation is made. The sentence is the expression of the mental formation. So when you meditate on a sentence, there are two methods. There is an active, ordinary external method of reflecting and trying to understand what these words mean, understand intellectually what the sentence means exactly—that is active meditation. You concentrate on these words and take the thought they express and try, through reasoning, deduction, analysis, to understand what it means.

There is another method, more direct and deep; it is to take this mental formation, this combination of words with the thought they represent, and to gather all your energy of attention on it, compelling yourself to concentrate all your strength on that formation. For instance, instead of concentrating all your energies on something you see physically, you take that thought and concentrate all your energies on that thought—in the mind, of course.

And then, if you are able to concentrate the thought sufficiently and stop it from vacillating, you pass quite naturally from the thought expressed by the word to the idea which is behind and which could be expressed in other words, other forms. The characteristic of the idea is the power to clothe itself in many different thoughts. And when you have achieved this, you have already gone much deeper than by merely understanding the words. Naturally, if you continue to concentrate and know how to do it, you can pass from the idea to the luminous force that is behind. Then you enter a much vaster and deeper domain. But that asks for some training. But still, that is the very principle of meditation.

If you are able to go deep enough, you find the Principle and the Force behind the idea, and that gives you the power of realisation. This is how those who take meditation as a means of spiritual devleopment are able to unite with the Principle which is behind things and obtain the power to act on these things from above.

But even without going so far—that implies a rather hard discipline, does it, a long-standing habit—you can pass quite easily from the thought of the idea, and that gives you a light and an understanding in the mind which enables you, in your turn, to express the idea in any form. An idea can be expressed in many different forms, in many different thoughts, just as when you come down to a more material level, a thought can be expressed through many different words. Going downwards, towards expression, that is, spoken or written expression, there are many different words and different formulas which may serve to express a thought, but this thought is only *one* of the forms of thought which can express the idea, the idea behind, and this idea itself, if it is followed deeply, has behind it a principle of spirtual knowledge and power which can then spread and act on the manifestation.

When you have a thought you look for words, don't you, and then you try to arrange these words to express your thought; you can use many words to express a thought, you tell yourself, "No, look, if I put this word instead of that, it would express what I am thinking much better." That is what you learn when you are taught style, how to write.

But when I give you a written sentence which has the power to express a thought and tell you to concentrate on it, then, through this thought-form you can go back to the idea behind, which can be expressed in many different thoughts. It is like a great hierarchy: there is a Principle right at the top, which itself is not the only one, for you can go still higher up; but this Principle can be expressed in ideas, and these ideas can be expressed in a great number of thoughts and this great number of thoughts can make use of many languages and an even greater number of words.

When I give you a thought it is simply to help you to concentrate. . . . There are schools which put an object in front of you, a flower or a stone, or any object, and then you sit around it and concentrate on it and your eyes go like this (*Mother squints*) until you become the object. That too is a method of concentration. By gazing steadily like that, without moving, you finally pass into the thing you are gazing at. But you must not begin to gaze at all kinds of things: only gaze steadily at that. That gives you a look . . . it makes you squint.

All this is to learn concentration, that's all. (9-381,382,383)

Concentration

Sometimes we look fixedly at a point; one forgets everything at that moment and if there is a noise one is disturbed. What is this state?

Concentration! It is exactly the very principle of concentration. Can you do it spontaneously?

Yes, many times.

Indeed, that's very good!

Yes, Sweet Mother, but what I thought at that moment I cannot capture.

Ah! . . . If you are suddenly pulled out from it, thought vanishes?

Yes.

That's because you enter a state of consciousness which is different from your ordinary state of consciousness and probably the link between the two is not established very well. That takes time. It is as though one had to build a bridge. Otherwise one takes a sudden jump to one side or the other, and then in jumping one forgets what was there. One leaves behind the experience one had. But if the thing is done methodically, that is, if every day one keeps a particular time for this, and meditates for ten or fifteen minutes in order to establish a contact between that and the outer life, well, after some time one succeeds and then one remembers, and this becomes very useful. It is very useful. And if your power of concentration is complete, them there is not a problem you cannot solve—I don't mean arithmetic problems (*laughter*), I mean problems about leading one's life, about decisions to be taken, psychological problems which need solving. There is not one that can resist this power of concentration.

And in fact it is very convenient to take a point: one looks steadily at the point, and so steadily that at a certain moment one becomes the point. One is no longer somebody looking at the point; one is the point. And then, if you continue with sufficient strength and quietness, without anything disturbing you, you may suddenly find yourself before a door which opens and you pass to the other side. And then you have the relevation.

Since when have you been doing this? This has always happened? Or is it recent?

I don't know.

You don't know? Perhaps you were doing it and were not aware of it! (5-399,400)

Concentration on a Problem

Yes, it is exactly that: it depends on the degree of concentration. If you observe yourself, you will notice this quite well: when it does not come, it is because of a kind of haziness in the brain, something cloudy, like a fog somewhere, and then you are there as in a dream. You push forward trying to find it, and it is as though you were pushing into cottonwool, you do not see clearly there; and so nothing comes. You may remain in that state for hours.

Concentration consists precisely in removing the cloud. You gather together all the elements of your intelligence and fix them on one point, and then you do not even try actively to find the thing. All that you do is to concentrate in such a way as to see only the problem—but seeing not only its surface, seeing it in its depth, what it conceals. If you are able to gather together all your mental energies, bringing them to a point which is fixed on the enunciation of the problem, and you stay there, fixed, as though you were about to drill a hole in the wall, all of a sudden it will come. And this is the only way. If you try: Is it this, is it that, is it this, is it that? . . . You will never find anything or else you will need hours. You must get your mental forces to a point with strength enough to pierce through the words and strike upon the thing that is behind. There is a thing to be found; swoop down upon it.

And it is always the days you are a little hazy that it becomes difficult. You are hazy: as though there is something you seem to catch and which escapes you.

Natually, if it is materially impossible—you do not have to deal with monsters! I believe your teachers are reasonable enough and if you go to them and say, "Well, I could not do it, I had no time, I did what I could, I did not have the time", they won't scold you, I don't think so. But here ninety-nine times out of a hundred, it is a kind of half inertia of the mind which makes you think that you have too much work. If you observe yourself, you will find out that there is always something which pulls this way, something which pulls that way and then this kind of haziness as though you were living in cottonwool, in the clouds: nothing is clear.

The usefulness of work is nothing else but that: to crystalise this mental power. For, what you learn (unless you put it in practice by some work or deeper studies), half of what you learn, at least, will vanish, disappear with time. But it will leave behind one thing: the capacity of crystallising your thought, making something clear out of it, something precise, exact and organised. And that is the true usefulness of work: to organise your cerebral capacity. If you remain in your hazy movement in that kind of cloudy fluidity, you may labour for years, it will be quite useless to you; you will not come out of it more intelligent than when you entered it. But if you are able, even for half an hour, to concentrate your attention on things that seem to you of very little interest, like a rule of grammar, for example (the rules of grammar are some of the dry things I was speaking about, there are other things much more arid, but indeed the rules of grammar are sufficiently arid), if you take one of them and try to understand it—not learn it by heart and apply mechanically what you have learnt by heart, that will be of no use—but try to understand the thought behind the words: "Why was this rule formulated in this way?" and try to find out your own formula for the thing; that is so interesting. "Why has this gentleman who wrote this rule written it in this way? (5-126,127)

Practical Value of Concentration

Moreover, whatever you may want to do in life, one thing is absolutely indispensable and at the basis of *everything*, the capacity of concentrating the attention. If you are able to gather together the rays of attention and consciousness on one point and can maintain this concentration with a persistent will, *nothing* can resist it—whatever it may be, from the most material physical development to the highest spiritual one. But this discipline must be followed in a constant and, it may be said, imperturbable way; not that you should always be concentrated on the same thing—that's not what I mean, I mean learning to concentrate.

And materially, for studies, sports, all physical or mental development, it is absolutely indispensable. And the value of an individual is proportionate to the value of his attention.

And from the spiritual point of view it is still more important. There is *no* spiritual obstacle which can resist a penetrating power of concentration. For instance, the discovery of the psychic being, union with the inner Divine, opening to the higher spheres, *all* can be obtained by an intense and obstinate power of concentration—but one must learn how to do it.

There is nothing in the human or even in the superhuman field, to which the power of concentration is not the key.

You can be the best athlete, you can be the best student, you can be an artistic, literary or scientific genius, you can be the greatest saint with that faculty. And everyone has in himself a tiny little beginning of it—it is given to everybody, but people do not cultivate it. (9-360,361)

Receiving Energy

Mother reads her article "Concentration and Dispersion" (*On Education*), then comments on it:,

To solve a problem, to learn a lesson, a lot of concentration and attention is needed, everyone knows that—an intellectual attention and concentration. But concentration is not only an intellectual thing, it may be found in all the activities of the being, including bodily activities. The control over the nerves should be such as would allow you a complete concentration on what you are doing and, through the very intensity of your concentration, you acquire an immediate response to external touches. To attain this concentration you need a conscious control of the energies.

Are you conscious of the energies you receive and those you spend?

One is more or less conscious of the energy one spends, especially when one wastes it too much! It is a question here of the constant exchange between receiving and spending! Before the age of reason, little children receive a lot of energy and they spend it lavishly, without thinking, and this allows them to play for hours together without getting tired. But gradually, as thought develops, one begins to measure and calculate the energy spent—usually this is futile, for unless you have the knowledge of the process of receiving energy, it is better to spend freely what you get than let it stagnate within you.

First, you must become conscious of the receiving of energies, their passing into your being and their expenditure. Next, you must have a sort of higher instinct which tells you whence the most favourable energies come; then you put yourself in contact with them through thought, through stillness or any other process—there are many. You must know what energy you want, whence it comes, of what it is composed. Later comes the control of the energy received. Ninety per cent of men do not absorb enough energy or they take in too much and do not assimilate what they take—as soon as they have had a sufficient dose they immediately throw it out by becoming restless, talking, shouting, etc. You must know how to keep within you the received energy and concentrate it fully on the desired activity and not on anything else. If you can do this, you won't need to use your will. You need only gather together all the energies received and use them consciously, concentrate with the maximum attention in order to do everything you want.

And you must know how to give a real value to what you *want* to do—what the higher part of your being wants to do—for to do what one *likes* to do is not difficult. (4-4,5)

Notes to Chapter 4

[1] Every evening, before meditation or the talks, Mother used to distribute groundnuts to the children of the "Green Group", in the adjoining playground.

5

PROGRESS

We have an innate urge for progress. We may not understand the reason for it or what it is we are progressing towards but the impetus is there nonetheless. As we become more conscious, that is, as we begin to understand our purpose in life and of the planet, our progress can accelerate, especially if we make a commitment. We can organize our life around a central purpose. Aspiration, sincerity, faith, unselfishness and resoluteness provide the foundation for this progress.

We Are Privileged to be Present at the Birth of a New World

What is indispensable in every case is the *ardent* will for progress, the willing and joyful renunciation of all that hampers the advance: to throw far away from oneself all that prevents one from going forward, and to set out in the unknown with the ardent faith that this is the truth of tomorrow, *inevitable*, which must necessarily come, which nothing, nobody, no bad will, even that of Nature, can prevent from becoming a reality—perhaps of a not too distant future—a reality which is being worked out now and which those who know how to change, how not to be weighed down by old habits, will *surely* have the good fortune not only to see but to realise.

People sleep, they forget, they take life easy—they forget, forget all the time. . . . But if we could remember . . . that we are at an exceptional hour, a *unique* time, that we have this immense good fortune, this invaluable privilege of being present at the birth of a new world, we could easily get rid of everything that impedes and hinders our progress.

So, the most important thing, it seems, is to remember

this fact; even when one doesn't have the tangible experience, to have the certainty of it and faith in it; to remember always, to recall it constantly, to go to sleep with this idea, to wake up with this perception; to do all that one does with this great truth as the background, as a constant support, this great truth that we are witnessing the birth of a new world.

We can participate in it, we can become this new world. And truly, when one has such a marvellous opportunity, one should be ready to give up everything for its sake. (9-158,159)

Everyday Miracles

My child, why do you put this in the future?

There have already been, for years, extraordinary, fantastic consequences in the world. But to see this, one must have a little knowledge; otherwise one takes them for quite normal and ordinary things—because one doesn't even know how they happen.

So perhaps this will be exactly the same thing; there are likely to be tremendous changes, fantastic actions, and, well, people will say, "But this—naturally, it is like that", because they don't know how it comes about.

An action in the world?—It is constant. It is something which spreads and acts everywhere, gives out everywhere new impulsions, new orientations, new ideas, new acts of will—everywhere. But still, as one does not see how it happens, one thinks it "quite natural", as they say.

It is quite natural, but with another naturalness than that of ordinary physical Nature.

Indeed, it is quite logical to say that one must be conscious of the Spirit to be able to perceive the work of the Spirit. If you are not conscious of the Spirit, how will you be able to see it at work? Because the result of what the Spirit does is necessarily material in the materialworld; and as it is material, you find it quite natural. What do you know of what Nature does, and what do you know of what the Spirit does? All that Nature does—I am speaking of physical Nature—we know very little about it, almost nothing, since we have to constantly learn things which upset all that we thought we knew before. And so, how to distinguish between what is purely the work of Nature and the work of the Spirit through Nature? One should know how to distinguish the one from the other. And how to distinguish them when one's consciousness is not quite limpid and sure of what the Spirit is? How to recognise It, and how to see Its Work? This seems to me very simple logic.

The world will go on. Things will happen. And perhaps there will be a handful of men who will know how they were done. That's all.

And if today one were suddenly precipitated, without any transition, into the world as it was, let us say, two or three thousand years ago; oh! even less than that perhaps—one or two thousand years ago—it would be such a suffocating contrast that probably very few people would be able to bear it. But as this came about "like that", with the amiable slowness of Nature, with all her fantasies, one finds it quite natural and doesn't even notice it.

It is not an image, it is not just fine words when it is said that if one enters the true consciousness, if one changes one's consciousness, well, the world itself changes for you. And it is not only an appearance or an impression: one sees differently than one does in the ordinary consciousness; relations are different, causes are different, effects are different. And instead of seeing only something which is not transparent—one cannot see what's behind, it is a surface, a crust; it is only this one sees and one can't even see what moves it, what makes it exist—everything is turned inside out, and it is that which appears artificial and unreal, and almost inexistent. And so, when one sees things in this way, normally, you know, without straining oneself, without having to practise meditation and concentration and make strenuous efforts to see things like this, when it is one's normal, natural vision, then one understands things in a completely different way—naturally, the world is different!

There is a short preliminary passage which is indispensable, and those who have made this little preliminary journey, well, there are all sorts of things, all sorts of speculations and questions which they can no longer ask themselves. (8-10,11,12)

Purpose of the Earth

But for our part, we are beginning from where he [Sri Aurobindo] has shown, from the purely intellectual point of view, what the purpose of existence is, and he formulates it like this: "the central significant motive of the terrestrial existence." For he is not concerned with the entire universe, he has taken terrestrial life, that is, our life here on Earth, as a symbolic and concentrated representation of the purpose of the entire universe. In fact, according to very old traditions, the Earth, from the deeper spiritual point of view, has been created as a symbolic concentration of universal life so that the work of transformation may be done more easily, in a limited, concentrated "space"—so to say—where all the elements of the problem are gathered together so that, in the concentration, the action may be more total and effective. So here he speaks only of terrestrial existence, but we can understand that it is a symbolic existence, that is, that it *represents* a universal action. It is a symbolic, concentrated representation. And he says that "the central motive", that is, the purpose of terrestrial existence is to awaken, to develop and finally to reveal in a total manifestation the Spirit which is hidden at the centre of Matter and impels this Matter *from within* outwards towards a progressive development which will liberate the Spirit working from within.

So, in the outer appearances as you see them, at first you find the mineral kingdom with stones, earth, minerals which to us, in our outer consciousness, appear absolutely unconscious. Yet, behind this unconsciousness there is the life of the Spirit, the consciousness of the Spirit, which is completely hidden, which is as if asleep—though that is only an appearance—and which works from within in order gradually to transform this Matter that is completely inert in appearance, so that its organisation may lend itself more and more to the manifestation of consciousness. (9-209)

Understanding Life

. . . they try to fill this by distraction, they become absolutely useless, and when they reach the end they have wasted their whole existence, all their possibilities—and everything is lost. This you will see: take a thousand men, out of them at least nine hundred and ninety are in this condition. It happens that they are born in circumstances or certain others, and they try, you see, to pass their time as well as they can, to be bored as little as possible, to suffer as little as possible, to have as good a time as possible; and everything is dull, lifeless, useless, stupid, and absolutely without any result. There, then. This is the majority of human beings, and they don't even think . . . they don't even ask themselves, "But indeed, why am I here? Why is there an earth? Why are there men? Why do I live?" No, all these things are absolutely uninteresting. The only interesting thing is to try to eat well, to have good fun, be nicely distracted, well married, have children, earn money and have all the advantages one can get from the point of view of desires, and above all, above all not to think, not reflect, not ask any questions, and avoid all trouble. Yes, and then get out of it like that, without too many catastrophes. This is the general condition; this is what men call being reasonable. And in this way the world can turn around indefinitely for eternity, it will never progress. And this is why all these are like ants; they come, crawl, die, go away, come back, crawl again, die again, and so on. And it can last for eternities like this. Fortunately there are some who do the work of all the others, but it's only these who will make everything change one day.

So the first problem is to know on which side one wants to be on: on the side of those who are doing something or the side of those who do nothing; on the side of those who, perhaps, will be able to understand what life is, and do what is necessary for this life to culminate in something, or else of those who hardly care to understand anything at all and try to pass their time in having as few botherations as possible. Above all, no botherations! (7-314)

From Semi-Conscious to Conscious

No. . . . And I could ask many others still. I know very well. Only those who have come after having had some experience of life and came because they wanted to come, and had a conscious reason for coming, they can of course tell me, "I came because of that", and that would be at least a partial explanation. The truest, deepest reason may still elude them, that is, what they specially have to realise in the Work. That already requires having passed through many stages on the path.

Essentially, it is only when one has become aware of one's soul, has been identified with one's psychic being that one can see in a single flash the picture of one's individual development through the ages. Then indeed one begins to know . . . but not before. Then, indeed, I assure you it becomes very interesting. It changes one's position in life.

There is such a great difference between feeling vaguely, having a hesitant impression of something, of a force, a movement, an impulse, an attraction, of something which drives you in life—but it is still so vague, so uncertain, it is hazy—there is such a difference between this and having a clear vision, an exact perception, a total understanding of the meaning of one's life. And only then does one begin to see things as they are, not before. Only then can one follow the thread of one's destiny and clearly see the goal and the way to reach it. But that happens only through successive inner awakenings, like doors opening suddenly on new horizons—truly, a new birth into a truer, deeper, more lasting consciousness.

Until then you live in a cloud, gropingly, under the weight of a destiny which at times crushes you, gives you the feeling of having been made in a certain way and being unable to do anything about it. You are under the burden of an existence which weighs you down, makes you crawl on the ground instead of rising above and seeing all the threads, the guiding threads, the threads which bind different things into a single movement of progression towards a realisation that grows clear.

One must spring up out of this half-consciousness which is usually considered quite natural—this is your "normal" way of being and you do not even draw back from it sufficiently to be able to see and wonder at this incertitude, this lack of precision; while, on the contrary, to know that one is seeking and to seek consciously, deliberately, *steadfastly* and methodically, this indeed is the exception, almost "abnormal" condition. And yet only in this way does one begin to truly live. (9-18,19)

Finding One's Purpose in Life

Perhaps his birth is the result of this choice; generally it is like that. But at any time at all in his life this can happen. Yet for those who are predestined it is before birth; usually they come to earth with an intention and a specific purpose.

You would like to know very much if this has happened to you, yes? (*Laughter*) Well, try—try to find out: have this inner aspiration, concentrate, and then try. If you get a result, tell me; I shall tell you if it is right. (8-27)

Progress for the Love of the Effort for Progress

As with everything in yoga, the effort for progress must

be made for the love of the effort for progress. The joy of effort, the aspiration for progress must be enough in themselves, quite independent of the result. Everything one does in yoga must be done for the joy of doing it, and not in view of the result one wants to obtain. . . . Indeed, in life, always, in all things, the result does not belong to us. And if we want to keep the right attitude, we must act, feel, think, strive spontaneously, for *that* is what we must do, and not in view of the result to be obtained. (9-316)

Inner Chaos

And in the head?

Ah! in the head, it is all the perversions of thought, all the treacheries—treacheries, there is a huge number of them: one betrays one's soul so often and so persistently, it is frightful—all the decisions, the points of view and favourable explanations, as I was telling you, and then a kind of habit of criticising . . . What one doesn't want to hear, when there is something higher which makes you feel your fault, there is a habit of immediately finding an explanation and a severe criticism of the idea or thought; or else some people turn it into ridicule; there are people who immediately oppose it with another idea or some commonplace notion or other. You can't imagine the bazaar there is in the head! It is something terrible. If you were to look really objectively at what is going on in there, it is frightful—before you put some order, see clearly, arrange all that, see that two contradictory ideas are not lined up parallel.

I know a large number of people who shelter in their minds contradictory ideas, not organised or synthesized—there is no question of a synthesis for them—but like . . . an almost fraternal cohabitation among things which are mortally opposed, that is, ideas which cannot lodge together. You can arrange them in a vast synthesis but that of course is a work of a higher order; yet two things, two ideas which have absolutely contradictory consequences in action and are absolutely contradictory explanations of the same fact . . . and these two things are there, side by side, they are even sometimes so close that one feels they are joined and live together without being troubled by the ridiculousness of their association.

I should one day give you a series of examples. Very often I tell you this, I have never given any examples; but one day I shall collect a number of examples for you and then give them to you. You will see this; if it were not sad it would be funny. Most men who have this don't even notice it, it does not trouble them. If you have some ideas about things—you should surely have some ideas about things, about the world, about life, about the purpose of existence, the aim of existence, the future realisation; in fact you do have many ideas—well, try this little game one day: put all these ideas before yourself, like this, and then arrange them; you will see how easy it will be, and you will perhaps have much fun; you will find surprising things.

Already, this work alone, just this work of bringing them out, of simply putting them side by side in front of you, all the ideas you have on any subject whatever, as though you were obliged to write them out as an exercise—you see, a composition you are asked to write: "What do you think of this thing, this subject?" and you are obliged to make a draft of it—put all the ideas side by side, and you will see, it will be amusing. Unless you are in the habit of having a central idea, if possible a fixed central truth around which you arrange all the ideas, you organise them in a logical order with the right relation between each of them, each one in its place, and you make a kind of monument of it—if you have never done this and you try to read in your mind, you will see something there, really. In fact, I tell you, if it were not sad it would be very funny. One can't imagine to what an extent one can, within the space of an hour, think about the most contradictory things, and without any astonishment.

It is a good exercise to put it down: All right, I am going to write a short essay on "What is . . . (take this, take anything at all, it doesn't matter), what is the goal life aims at?" Or else "What is the purpose of existence upon earth?" or "Why are men born in order to die?" anything at all, take things like that. I don't say take "Why did you play football today and will play basketball tomorrow?" no, not things like that, because these you can always explain. I am speaking to you of things a little more general. Put that before you and then line up the ideas you have on the subject, you will see it will be amusing. (7-90,91,92)

Ridding Oneself of Impulses and Desires

All forces upon earth tends towards expressing themselves. These forces come with the object of manifesting themselves and if you place a barrier and refuse expression, they may try to beat against the barrier for a time, but in the end, they will tire themselves out and not being manifested, they will withdraw and leave you quiet.

So you must never say: "I shall first purify my thought, purify my body, purify my vital and then later I shall purify my action." That is the normal order, but it never succeeds. The effective order is to begin from the outside: "The very first thing is that I do not do it, and afterwards, I desire it no longer and next I close my doors completely to all impulses: they no longer exist for me, I am now outside all that." This is the true order, the order that is effective. First, not to do it. And then you will no longer desire and after that it will go out of your consciousness completely. (5-214,215)

Ask the Divine

If, for example, one wants to know something or one needs guidance, or something else, how can one have it from the Divine, according to one's need?

By asking the Divine for it. If you do not ask Him, how can you have it?

If you turn to the Divine and have full trust and ask Him, you will get what you need—not necessarily what you imagine you need; but the true thing you need, you will get. But you must ask Him for it.

You must make the experiment sincerely; you must not endeavour to get it by all sorts of external means and then expect the Divine to give it to you, without even having asked Him. Indeed, when you want somebody to give you something, you ask him for it, don't you? And why do you expect the Divine to give it to you without your having asked Him for it?

In the ordinary consciousness the movement is just the opposite. You assume something, saying, "I need this, I need this relationship, I need this affection, I need this knowledge, etc. Well, the Divine ought to give it to me, otherwise He is not the Divine." That is to say, you reverse the problem completely.

First of all, you say, "I need." Do you know whether you truly need it or whether it is only an impression you have or a desire or quite an ignorant movement? First point: you know nothing about it.

Second point: it is precisely your own will you want to impose upon the Divine, telling Him, "I need this." And then you don't even ask Him for it: "Give it to me." You say, "I need it. Therefore, since I need it, it must come to me, quite naturally, spontaneously; it's the Divine's job to give me all that I need."

But if it so happens that truly you don't know what you need and it is merely an illusion and not a truth and that, into the bargain, you ask it from life around you and don't turn to the Divine, don't create any relationship between yourself and Him, don't think of Him or turn to Him with at least some sincerity in your attitude, then, as you ask nothing from Him, there is no reason for Him to give you anything. (8-122,123)

Organizing One's Life by Telling A Beautiful Story

You begin a story, then, when it is time to wake up, you put a full stop to the last sentence and come back into your body. And then the following night you start off again, reopen the page and resume your story during the whole time you are out; and then you arrange things well—they must be well arranged, it must be very beautiful. And when it is time to come back, you put a full stop once again and tell those things, "Stay very quiet till I return!" And you come back into your body. And you continue this every evening and write a book of wonderful fairy-tales—provided you remember them when you wake up.

But this depends on being in a quiet state during the day, doesn't it?

No, it depends on the candour of the child.

And on the trust he has in what happens to him, on the absence of the mind's critical sense, and a simplicity of heart, and a youthful and active energy—it depends on all that—on a kind of inner vital generosity: one must not be too egoistic, one must not be too miserly, nor too practical, too utilitarian—indeed there are all sorts of things one should not be . . . like children. And then, one must have a lively power of imagination, for—I seem to be telling you stupid things, but it is quite true—there is a world in which you are the supreme maker of forms: that is your own particular vital world. You are the supreme fashioner and you can make a marvel of your world if you know how to use it. If you have an artistic of poetic consciousness, if you love harmony, beauty, you will build there something marvellous which will tend to spring up into the material manifestation.

When I was small I used to call this "telling stories to oneself". It is not at all a telling with words, in one's head: it is a going away to this place which is fresh and pure, and . . . building up a wonderful story there. And if you know how to tell yourself a story in this way, and if it is truly beautiful, truly harmonious, truly powerful and well co-ordinated, this story will be realised in your life—perhaps not exactly in the form in which you created it, but as a more or less changed physical expression of what you made.

That may take years, perhaps, but your story will tend to organise your life.

But there are very few people who know how to tell a beautiful story; and then they always mix horrors in it, which they regret later.

If one could create a magnificent story without any horror in it, nothing but beauty, it would have a *considerable* influence on everyone's life. And this is what people don't know.

If one knew how to use this power, this creative power in the world of vital forms, if one knew how to use this while yet a child, a very small child . . . for it is then that one fashions his material destiny. But usually people around you, sometimes even your own little friends, but mostly parents and teachers, dabble in it and spoil everything for you, so well that very seldom does the thing succeed completely.

But otherwise, if it were done like that, with the spontaneous candour of a child, you could organise a wonderful life for yourself—I am speaking of the physical world.

The dreams of childhood are the realities of mature age. (8-118,119)

Having an Experience

. . . this does not mean that the intensity, the power of action and the force were not there—they were there, and probably in the best cases the utmost effect of the experience is produced before you begin to give it a comprehensible form.

I am speaking here of the best cases. I am not speaking of the innumerable cases of those who begin to have an experience and whose mind becomes curious, wakes up and says, "Oh! what is happening?" Then everything vanishes. Or maybe one catches the deformed tail of something which has lost all its force and all its reality. . . . The first thing to do is to teach your mind *not to stir*: "Above all, don't move! Above all, don't move, let the things develop fully without wanting to know what is happening; don't be stupid, keep quiet, be still, and wait. Your turn will always come too soon, never too late." It should be possible to live an experience for hours and for days together without feeling the need to formulate it to yourself. When one does that, one gets the full benefit from it. Then it works, it churns the nature, it transforms the cells—it begins its great work of transformation. But as soon as you begin to look and to understand and to formulate, it is already something that belongs to the past. (8-343)

Opportunities for Progress

With the touch of the divine Grace, how do difficulties become opportunities for progress?

Opportunities for progress? Yes! Well, this is something quite obvious. You have made a big mistake, you are in great difficulty: then, if you have faith, if you have trust in the divine Grace, if you really rely on It, you will suddenly realise that it is a lesson, that your difficulty or mistake is nothing else but a lesson and that it comes to teach you to find within yourself what needs to be changed, and with this help of the divine Grace you will discover in yourself what has to be changed. And you will change it. And so, from a difficulty you will have made great progress, taken a considerable leap forward. This, indeed, happens all the time. Only, you must be truly sincere, that is, rely on the Grace and let It work in you—not like this: one part of you asking to be helped and another resisting as much as it can, because it doesn't want to change . . . this is the difficulty.

All that he is saying, all the time, is: completely, totally, sincerely, without reserve. For there is one part of the being which has an aspiration, there is one part of the being which gives itself, and there are other parts—sometimes a small part, sometimes a big one which hides nicely, right at the bottom, and keeps absolutely quiet so that it may not be found out, but which *resists* with *all* its might, so as not to change.

And so one wonders . . . with, "Oh, I had such a beautiful aspiration, I had so much goodwill, I had such a great desire to change, and the, see, I cannot! Why?" Then, of course, your mental arrogance comes in and says, "I didn't get the response I deserved, the divine Grace doesn't help me, and I am left all alone to shift for myself", etc., etc.

It is not that. It is that hidden somewhere there is a tiny something which is well coiled up, in there, *doubled up, turned in* upon itself and well hidden, right at the bottom, as at the bottom of a box, which refuses to stir. So when the effort, the aspiration wane, die down, this springs up like that, gently, and then it wants to impose its will and it makes you do exactly what you did not want to do, what you had decided you would not do, and which you do without knowing how or why! Because that thing was there, it had its turn—for small things, big things, for the details, even for the direction of life.

There are people who see clearly, who know so well what they ought to do, and who feel that they can't. . . . They don't know why. It is nothing else but that. There is a little spot which doesn't want to change and this little spot awaits its hour. And the day it is allowed, through laxity, fatigue, somnolence, through a little inertia, allowed to show itself, it will show itself with all concentrated, accumulated energy, and will make you do, will make you say, make you feel, make you act *ex-actly* contrary to what you had decided to do! And you will stand there: "Ah, how discouraging this is! . . . " Then some people say, "Fate!" They think it is their fate. It is not fate, it is themselves! . . . It is that they don't have, haven't used, the light, the searchlight. They have not turned the searchlight into the small hidden corners of their being, they haven't discovered what was well hidden. They have left it there, and then have done this (*Mother turns away her head*) so as not to see it. How many times one suddenly feels one is on the point of catching something, "Hup!" It hurts a little. . . . It is troublesome. . . . So one thinks of something else, and that's all! The opportunity has gone. One must wait for another occasion, again commit a few stupidities, before being able to find an opportunity to catch the thing by the tail, like this, or by the ear or the nose, and hold it firmly and say, "No! you won't hide any longer now, I see you as you are, and you must either get out or change!" (6-242,243)

Sincerity to Perceive Inner Guidance

Before undertaking any action one tries to know whether the impulse comes from the Mother or not, but generally one doesn't have enough discernment to know it and yet one acts. Can one know from the result of the action whether it came from the Mother or not?

One does not have the discernment because one does not care to have it! Listen, I don't think there is a single instance in which one does not find within oneself something very clear, but you must sincerely want to know—we always come back to the same thing—you must sincerely want it. The first condition is not to begin thinking about the subject and building all sorts of ideas: opposing ideas, possibilities, and entering into a formidable mental activity. First of all, you must put the problem as though you were putting it to someone else, then keep silent, remain like that, immobile. And then, after a little while you will see that at least three different things may happen, sometimes more. Take the case of an intellectual, one who acts in accordance with the indications of his head. He has put the problem and he waits. Well, if he is indeed attentive, he will notice that there is (the chronological order is not absolute, it may come in different order) at first (what is most prominent in an intellectual) a certain idea: "If I do that in this way, it will be all right; it must be like that", that is to say, a mental construction. A second thing which is a kind of impulse: "That will have to be done. That is good, it must be done." Then a third which does not make any noise at all, does not try to impose itself on the others, but has the tranquility of a certitude—not very active, not giving a shock, not pushing to action, but something that knows and is very quiet, very still. This will not contradict the others, will not come and say,"No, that's wrong": it says simply, "See, it is like this", that's all, and then it does not insist. The majority of men are not silent enough or attentive enough to be aware of it, for it makes no noise. But I assure you it is there in everybody and if one is truly sincere and succeeds in being truly quiet, one will become aware of it. The thinking part begins to argue,"But after all, this thing will have this consequence and that thing will have that consequence, and if one does this . . . " and this, and that . . . and its noise begins again. The other (the vital) will say, "Yes, it *must* be done like that, it *must* be done, you don't understand, it *must*, it is indispensable." There! then you will know. And according to your nature you will choose either the vital impulse or the mental leading, but very seldom do you say quite calmly, "Good, it is this I am going to do, whatever happens", and even if you don't like it very much. But it is always there. I am sure that it is there even in the murderer before he kills, you understand, but his outer being makes such a lot of noise that it never occurs to him to listen. But it is always there, always there. In every circumstance, there is in the depth of every being, just this little (one can't call it "voice", for it makes no sound) this little indication of the divine Grace, and sometimes to obey it requires a tremendous effort, for all the rest of the being opposes it violently, one part with the conviction that what it thinks is true, another with all the power, the strength of its desire. But don't tell me that one can't know, for that is not true. One can know. But one does not always know what is necessary, and sometimes, if one knows what is to be done, well, one finds some excuse or other for not doing it. One tells oneself, "Oh! I am not so sure, after all, of this inner indication; it does not assert itself with sufficient force for me to trust it." But if you were quite indifferent, that is, if you had no desire, either mental or vital or physical desire, you would know with certainty that it is that which must be done and nothing else. What comes and gets in the way is preference—preferences and desires. Every day one may have hundreds and hundreds of examples. When people begin to say, "Truly I don't know what to do", it always means that they have a preference. But as here in the Ashram they know there is something else and as at times they have been a little attentive, they have a vague sensation that it is not quite that: "It is not quite that, I don't feel quite at ease." Besides, you were saying a while ago that it is the result which gives you the indication; it has even been said (it has been written in books) that one judges the divine Will by the results! all that succeeds has been willed by the Divine; all that doesn't, well, He has not willed it! This is yet again one of those stupidities big as a mountain. It is a mental simplification of the problem, which is quite comic. That's not it. If one can have an indication (in proportion to one's sincerity), it is uneasiness, a little uneasiness—not a great uneasiness, just a little uneasiness.

Here, you know, you have another means, quite simple (I don't know why you do not use it, because it is quite elementary); you imagine I am in front of you and then ask yourself, "Would I do this before Mother, without difficulty, without any effort, without something holding me back?" That will never deceive you. If you are sincere you will know immediately. That would stop many people on the verge of folly. (4-386,387,388)

The Effectiveness of Faith

That is not enough. A mental resolution is not enough, no. There are subtle reactions in your body which do not obey the mental resolution, it is not enough. Something else is needed.

Other regions must be contacted. A power higher than the mind's is needed.

And from this point of view, all that is in the mind is always subject to inner questioning. You take a resolution but you can be sure that something will always come in which perhaps may not openly fight this resolution but will question its effectiveness. It is enough, you see, to be subject to the least doubt for the resolution to lose half its effect. If at the same time as you say "I want", there is something silently lurking, somewhere behind, in the background, something which asks itself, "What will the result be?" that is enough to ruin everything.

This play of the mind's working is extremely subtle and no ordinary human means can succeed in controlling it perfectly. For instance, this is well known among people who practise yoga and want to control their body: if through an assiduous yogic effort they have succeeded in controlling something in themselves—a particular weakness of the body, an opening to a certain disequilibrium—if they have managed to do this and had some result, for instance the disappearance of this disequilibrium for a very long time, for years, well, if one day at a particular moment, suddenly, the thought crosses their mind that "Ah! now it is done", the very next minute it returns. That is enough. For it proves that they have come into contact with the vibrations of the thing they had rejected, on a plane where they are vulnerable, the plane of thought, and that for some reason or other in the play of forces, they are open, and it comes back.

This is something very well known in yoga. The simple fact of observing the victory one has gained—observing it mentally, you see, thinking about it—is enough to destroy the effect of the yoga which may have existed for years. A mental silence strong enough to prevent all outer vibrations from coming in, is indispensable. Well, that is something so difficult to achieve that one must really have passed from what Sri Aurobindo calls "the lower hemisphere" to the higher, exclusively spiritual hemisphere, for it not to happen.

No, it is not in the mental field that the victories are won. It is impossible. It is open to all influences, all contradictory currents. All the mental constructions one makes carry their own contradiction with them. One can try to overrule it or make it as harmless as possible, but it exists, it is there, and at the slightest weakness or lack of vigilance or inadvertance, it enters, and destroys all the work. Mentally, one arrives at very few results, and they are always mixed. Something else is needed. One must pass from the mind into the domain of faith or of a higher consciousness, to be able to act with safety.

It is quite obvious that one of the most powerful means for acting on the body is faith. People who have a simple heart, not a very complicated mind—simple people, you see—who don't have a very great, very complicated mental development but have a very deep faith, have a great power of action over their bodies, very great. That is why one is quite surprised at times: "Here's a man with a great realisation, an exceptional person, and he is a slave of the smallest physical things, while this man, well, he is so simple and looks so uncouth, but he has a great faith and goes through difficulties and obstacles like a conqueror!"

I don't say that a highly cultured man can't have faith, but it is more difficult, for there is always this mental element which contradicts, discusses, tries to understand, which is difficult to convince, who wants proofs. His faith is less pure. It is necessary, then, to pass on to a higher degree in the evolutionary spiral, pass from the mental to the spiritual; then, naturally, faith takes on a quality of a very high order. But I mean that in daily life, ordinary life, a very simple man who has a very ardent faith can have a mastery over his body . . . (9-124,125)

Active Faith

Later—much later—one day, looking back, we may see that everything that happened, even what seem to us the worst, was a Divine Grace to make us advance on the way; and then we become aware that the personal effort too was a grace. But before reaching that one, one has to advance much, to struggle much, sometimes even to suffer a great deal.

To sit down in inert passivity and say, "If I am to have faith I shall have it, the Divine will give it to me", is an attitude of laziness, of unconsciousness and almost of bad-will.

For the inner flame to burn, one must feed it; one must watch over the fire, throw into it the fuel of all the errors one wants to get rid of, all that delays the progress, all that darkens the path. If one doesn't feed the fire, it smoulders under the ashes of one's unconsciousness and inertia, and then, not years but lives, centuries will pass before one reaches the goal.

One must watch over one's faith as one watches over the birth of something *infinitely* precious, and protect it very carefully from everything that can impair it.

In the ignorance and darkness of the beginning, faith is the most direct expression of the Divine Power which comes to fight and conquer. (9-352)

Understanding God's Grace

What I would like to bring home to you is that the problem is extremely complicated and subtle, and that at times the direction of the movement can be altered a little; at other times, the movement can be reversed; and at still others just the consequences and the inner attitude with regard to the movement alone can be changed. And naturally men see all these things in a too simplified way and translate all this by their prayer to God: they say, in one case, "God has given me what I asked from him", in another case, "He has refused me." And so, that's that. That is how they understand and it is sheer stupidity. To know how it happens, you must have a general collective consciousness, at least as wide as the earth. That is the minimum. To understand truly one must have a universal consciousness. Then you can understand. For, I have said it somewhere in what I was reading today; I have said that all things are interdependent and there is neither any "beginning" nor any "end". Where do you put the beginning?[1] . . . To understand that, you have to go beyond the earth-bound consciousness, you have to enter a universal consciousness. Then you will be able to understand. (5-194)

Energy

How is it that as mental activities increase, the capacity to renew one's energies diminishes?

In adults mental activity tends to paralyse the spontaneous movement of exchange of energies. Till he is fourteen, every child, apart from a few rare exceptions, is a little animal; he renews his energies spontaneously like an animal by means of the same activities and exchanges. But the mind introduces a disequilibrium in the being; spontaneous action is replaced by something that wants to know, to regulate, to decide, etc., and to get back this capacity to renew spontaneously one's energies, one must rise to a higher rung above the instincts, that is, from ordinary mental activity one must pass direct into intuition.

> *"Yet there is a source of energy which, once discovered, never dries up, whatever the circumstances and the physical conditions in life. It is the energy that can be described as spiritual, that which is received not from below, from the depths of inconscience, but from above, from the supreme origin of men and the universe, from the all-powerful and eternal splendours of the superconscious. It is there, everywhere around us, penetrating everything and to enter into contact with it and receive it, it is sufficient to sincerely aspire for it, to open oneself to it in faith and confidence so as to enlarge one's consciousness for identifying it with the universal Consciousness."*
>
> "Energy Inexhaustible", *On Education*

(4-6,7)

Divine Will

How are we to know, you will ask, when it is the Divine Will that makes us act? The Divine Will is not difficult to recognise. It is unmistakable. You can know it without being very far on the path. Only you must listen to its voice, the small voice that is here in the heart. Once you are accustomed to listen, if you do anything that is contrary to the Divine Will, you feel an uneasiness. If you persist on the wrong tract, you get very much disturbed. (3-8)

Strengthening One's Will

Mother, how can one strengthen one's will?

Oh, as one strengthens muscles, by a methodical exercise. You take one little thing, something you want to do or don't want to do. Begin with a small thing, not something very essential to the being, but a small detail. And then, if, for instance, it is something you are in the habit of doing, you insist on it with the same regularity, you see, either not to do it or to do it—you insist on it and compel yourself to do it as you compel yourself to lift a weight—it's the same thing. You make the same kind of effort, but it is more of an inner effort. And after having taken little things like this—things relatively easy, you know—after taking these and suceeding with them, you can unite with a greater force and try a more complicated experiment. And gradually, if you do this regularly, you will end up by acquiring an independent and very strong will. (6-391)

The Divine Does Not Need Our Help, He Wants Our Consent

If these very people who are ready to give money for schools were told that there was a divine Work to be done, that the Divine has decided to do it in this particular way, even if they are convinced that it is indeed the Divine's Work, they refuse to give anything, for this is not a recognised form of beneficence—one doesn't have the satisfaction of having done something good! This is what I call ambition. I had instances of people who could give lakhs of rupees to open a hospital, for that gives them the satisfaction of doing something great, noble, generous. They glorify themselves, that's what I call ambition.

I knew a humorist who used to say: "It won't be so soon that the kingdom of God will come, for those poor philanthropists—what would remain for them? If humanity suffered no longer, the philanthropists would be without work." It is difficult to come out of the state in which it is unless it gives itself up to the Divine. All the virtues—you may glorify them—increase your self-satisfaction, that is, your ego; they do not help you truly to become aware of the Divine. It is the generous and wise people of this world who are the most difficult to convert. They are very satisfied with their life. A poor fellow who has done all sorts of stupid things all his life feels immediately sorry and says: "I am nothing, can do nothing. Make of me what You want." Such a one is more right and much closer to the Divine than one who is wise and full of his wisdom and vanity. He sees himself as he is.

The generous and wise man who has done much for humanity is too self-satisfied to have the least idea of changing. It is usually these people who say: "If indeed I had created the world, I wouldn't have made it like this, I would have created it much better than that", and they try to set right what the Divine has done badly! According to their picture, all this is stupid and useless. . . . It is not with that attitude that you can belong to the Divine. There will always be between you and Him the conscious ego of one's own intellectual superiority which judges the Divine and is sure of never being mistaken. For they are convinced that if they had made the world, they would not have committed all the stupidities that God has perpetrated.And all this comes from pride, vanity, self-conceit; and there is exactly the seed of that in people who want to serve humanity.

What are they going to give to humanity? Nothing at all! Even if they gave every drop of their blood, all the ideas in their head, all the money in their pocket, that could not change one individual, who is but a second of time in eternity. They believe they can serve eternity? There are even beings higher than man who have come, have brought the light, given their life, and that has not changed things much. So how can a little man, a microscopic being, truly help? It is pride. The argument given is: "If everyone did his best, all would go well." I don't think so and, even, it is impossible. In a certain way, each thing in the universe does its best. But that best doesn't come to anything at all. Unless everything changes, nothing will change. It is this best that must change. In the place of ignorance must be born knowledge and power and consciousness, othewise we shall always turn in a circle around the same stupidity.

You may open millions of hospitals, that will not prevent people getting ill. On the contrary, they will have every facility and encouragement to fall ill. We are steeped in ideas of this kind. This puts your conscience at rest: "I have come to the world, I must help others." One tells oneself: "How disinterested I am! I am going to help humanity." All this is nothing but egoism.

In fact, the first human being that concerns you is yourself. You want to diminish suffering, but unless you can change the capacity of suffering into a certitude of being happy, the world will not change. It will always be the same, we turn in a circle—one civilisation follows another, one catastrophe another; but the thing does not change, for there is something missing, something not there, that is the consciousness. (5-14,15)

Resoluteness on the Path

But if one leaves the path, it is even very difficult to find again. What is strange is that in leaving it one loses it. There are legends of this kind in all countries: of people who have left the path and then later searched for it and never found it again. It was as if it had vanished. They lost it and this truly is a very sad thing.

But when you are on the path, I said this—I was just saying it—when you are on the path, do not ever leave it. Wait a little, you can hesitate as long as you want before taking it; but the minute you set your foot on it, it is finished, don't leave it. Because this has consequences which can even extend to several lives. It is something very serious. That is why, besides, I never push anyone to take the path. You are quite a number of children here; I have never asked anyone—only those who came to me and told me, "I want it." And to these also, unless I am absolutely sure of them because it is written in their destiny that they have come for that, I always say, "Think about it, think, be quite sure that this is what you want and nothing else." And when they have reflected and decided, it is finished. One should no longer move away, one should go straight to the end. I mean, one should not leave the path any more. One should go forward at all costs and try not to stop too often on the way, because it is easier to continue even if it is hard, you see, than to begin all over again when one has stopped. A much greater effort is needed to get going again than to continue on the way. And you see, logically I should not say it, but I have already warned all who are here, I have told them, "Don't ever take lightly all the circumstances of each day, all the tiny little things of life, all the small events, you know; never take all this lightly." Never react with your lower being. Each time you are told to do something or not to do it—you are not told this very often, but each time you are told, before reacting think a little, try to find in yourself the part which reacts. Do not react just like that with what is most commonplace in you. Enter within yourself, try to find the best in yourself and with this you must react. *It is very important, it is very important.*

There are people who mark time for years because they haven't done this. There are others who seem to fly, so fast do they go, because they pay attention to this. And those who don't do that throw the blame always on the Divine. They accuse the Grace. They tell her, "It is You who deceived me, it is You who put me into difficulty, it is You who made me stumble, it is You who are a monster", not exactly in these words, but their thought is like this. And so, naturally, they make their case worse because they push away even the help they could have had in their difficulty. There we are.

I could tell you many more things, but it will come gradually. In any case, if you can keep within yourself a confidence, a candid trust which does not argue, and the sense of . . . yes, it is truly a kind of trust that what is done for you, in spite of all appearances, is always the best thing to lead you in the quickest way possible out of all your difficulties and towards the goal . . . if you can keep that strong in you, well, your path will become tremendously easier.

You will tell me that it is very difficult to keep it, but children keep it very well. They must have truly come upon particularly detestable parents to lose it; but if their parents are simply good enough, they keep this very well. Well, it is this attitude; if you can tell yourself, "Good, perhaps the divine Grace deserves our confidence", simply this, nothing else, you will avoid many difficulties, many. In fact this avoids many difficulties even in ordinary life, and many worries. And particularly here, if you can do that, well, you will see things which seemed formidably difficult dissolving suddenly like clouds. (6-444,445)

Doing the Impossible

> *"What I cannot do now is the sign of what I shall do hereafter. The sense of impossibility is the beginning of all possibilities. Because this temporal universe was a paradox and an impossibility, therefore the Eternal created it out of His being."*
>
> *Thoughts and Glimpses*, Cent. Vol. 16, p. 378

Do you know why this seems paradoxical to you? It is simply because Sri Aurobindo has not put in the guide marks of the thought, hasn't led you step by step from one thought to another. It is nothing else. It is almost elementary in its simplicity.

And I am simply going to ask you a question—but in fact I expect no answer—to tell you something very simple: When does something seem impossible to you?—It is when you try to do it. If you have never tried to do it, it would never have seemed impossible to you.

And how is it that you tried to do it?—Because it was somewhere in your consciousness. If it had not been in your consciousness, you would not have tried to do it; and the moment it is in your consciousness, it is quite obvious that it is something you will realise. That alone which is not in your consciousness you cannot realise. it's as simple as that!

Only, instead of telling you the thing in this way, Sri Aurobindo puts it in a way that stimulates your thought. That is the virtue of paradoxes, they compel you to think. (8-383)

Aspiration for the Transformation

It is for you to know whether this interests you more than everything else in the world. . . . There comes a moment when the body itself finds that there is *nothing in the world* which is so worth living for as this transformation; that there is nothing which can have as great an interest as this passionate interest of transformation. It is as though all the cells of the body were athirst for that Light which wants to manifest; they cry out for it, they find an intense joy in it and are *sure* of the Victory.

This is the aspiration that I am trying to communicate to you, and you will understand that everything else in life is dull, insipid, futile, worthless in comparison with that: the transformation in the Light. (9-191)

Relate to the Person's Soul, Not to the Body

But it is not like that, it is not a bottle into which one pours some liquid! It's not that!

Are you asking whether the body will keep its masculine or feminine form? Probably this will be left to the choice of the being who enters the house, the occupant. . . . Does it interest you very much, this difference? (*Laughter*)

> *You tell us that there won't be any difference, but so far there is still a great difference.*

From what point of view? If it is the physical appearance, I agree—and yet, not so much as all that, but still . . . From what point of view?

From the point of view of the idea of sex, that there are different sexes. That still exists.

The idea! But that's the fault of the person who thinks! One can very well dispense with thinking. You know, these very petty limits of thought are things which ought to disappear before you can even attempt to transform your body. If you still have these very petty ideas which are purely animal, there is not much hope that you could begin the least process for the transformation of your body. You must first transform your thought. . . . For that is something which is still crawling far down below. If you are not able to feel that a conscious and living being can be quite free, even in a certain definite form, from all feeling of sex, it . . . it means that you are still up to your neck in the original animality.

In the inner thought one feels it, but in the actuality of material life . . .

What about the actuality?

In the outer life I haven't yet realised that. In the inner . . .

You spend your time thinking about it?

But one may live twenty-four hours out of twenty-four without giving a single thought to this difference! You must really be hypnotised by this affair. Do you suppose that when I speak to you I think that you are a man and when I speak to Tara I think she is a woman?

Still there is a difference!

Ah! but it is not at all necessary.

In theory I understand.

In theory! What theory?

That there is no difference. But when I am in contact with someone, either I am speaking to a man or a woman.

Well, it's a great pity both for you and for the other person.

No, it is just the very opposite of what ought to happen! When you are in contact with someone and speaking with him, it is precisely to what surpasses all animality that you should speak; it is to the soul you must speak, never to the body. Even more is asked of you, for you are asked to address the Divine—not even the soul—the one Divine in every being, and to be conscious of that.

But if only one person is conscious and the other is a brute, what will happen?

If you alone are conscious? And what do you know about it? And how and on what plane do you judge that the other is not conscious?

His way of replying.

But perhaps he thinks the same of you!

Well, I tell you that so long as it is not the divine Presence you address when you speak to someone, it means you are not conscious of it in yourself. And then it's terribly presumptuous to judge what state the other person is in. What do you know about it? If you yourself are not conscious of the Divine in the other being, what right have you to say whether he is conscious of it or not? On what basis? Your small outer intelligence? But it knows nothing! It is quite incapable of perceiving anything whatever.

Unless your vision is *constantly* the vision of the Divine in all things, you have not only no right but no capacity to judge the state which others are in. And to pronounce a judgment on someone without having this vision spontaneously, effortlessly, is precisely an example of the mental presumptuousness of which Sri Aurobindo always spoke.

. . . And it so happens that one who has the vision, the consciousness, who is capable of seeing the truth in all things, never feels the need to judge anything whatever. For he understands everything and knows everything. Therefore, once and for all, you must tell yourselves that the moment you begin to judge things, people, circumstances, you are in the most total human ignorance.

In short, one could put it like this: when one understands, one no longer judges and when one judges, it means that one doesn't know.

Judging people is one of the first things which must be totally swept away from the consciousness before you can take even a step on the supramental path, because that is not a material progress or a bodily progress, it is only a very little progress of thought, mental progress. And unless you have swept your mind clean of all its ignorance, you cannot hope to take a step on the supramental path.

In fact, you have said something terrible. When you said, "I cannot speak to his soul if he is a brute", well, you have given yourself away . . . you have stuck a label on yourself. There you are.

All those who have truly and sincerely had the experience of the divine Presence, all those who have truly been in contact with the Divine, have always said the same thing: that sometimes, even often, it is in what is most decried by men, most despised by men, most condemned by human "wisdom", that one can see the divine light shining.

They are not mere words, they are living experiences. All these ideas of good and evil, good and bad, higher, lower, all these notions belong to the ignorance of the human mind, and if one really wants to come into contact with the divine life, one must liberate oneself totally from this ignorance, one must rise to a region of consciousness where these things have *no* reality. The feeling of superiority and inferiority completely disappears, it is replaced by something else which is of a very different nature—a sort of capacity for filtering appearances, penetrating behind masks, shifting the point of view.

And these are not words, it is altogether true that *everything* changes its appearance, totally, that life and things are completely different from what they appear to be.

All this contact, this ordinary perception of the world loses its reality completely. This is what appears unreal, fantastic, illusory, non-existent. There is something—something very material, very concrete, very physical—which becomes the reality of the being, and which has nothing incommon with the ordinary way of seeing. When one has this perception—the perception of the work of the divine force, of the movement being worked out behind the appearance, in the appearance, through the appearance—one begins to be ready to live something truer than the ordinary human falsehood. But not before.

There is no compromise, you see. It is not like a convalescence after an illness: you must change worlds. So long as your mind is real for you, your way of thinking something true for you, real, concrete, it proves that you are not there yet. You must first pass through to the other side. Afterwards you will be able to understand what I am telling you.

Pass through to the other side.

It is not true that one can understand little by little, it is not like that. This kind of progress is different. What is more true is that one is shut up in a shell, and inside it something is happening, like the chick in the egg. It is getting ready in there. It is in there. One doesn't see it. Something is happening in the shell, but outside one sees nothing. And it is only when all is ready that there comes the capacity to pierce the shell and to be born into the light of day.

It is not that one becomes more and more perceptible or visible: one is shut in—shut in—and for sensitive people there is even that terrible sensation of being compressed, of trying to pass through and then coming up against a wall. And then one knocks and knocks and knocks, and one can't go through.

And so long as one is there, inside, one is in the falsehood. And only on the day when by the Divine Grace one can break the shell and come out into the Light, is one free.

This may happen suddenly, spontaneously, quite unexpectedly.

I don't think one can go through gradually. I don't think it is something which slowly wears and wears away until one can see through it. I haven't had an instance of this so far. There is rather a kind of accumulation of power inside, an intensification of the need, and an endurance in the effort which becomes free from all fear, all anxiety, all calculation; a need so imperative that one no longer cares for the consequences.

One is like an explosive that nothing can resist, and one bursts out from one's prison in a blaze of light.

After that one can no longer fall back again.

It is truly a new birth. (9-131,132,133,134,135,136)

Recognize the Value of Others

"To be modest"

This is to take oneself at one's true worth.

Generally people pass from an excessive appreciation of their personal value to an equally excessive discouragement. One day they say, "I am wonderful", and the next day, "Oh! I am good for nothing, I can do nothing." That is like a pendulum, isn't it? There is nothing more difficult than knowing exactly what one is; one must neither overrate oneself nor depreciate oneself, but understand one's limits and know how to advance towards the ideal set before oneself. There are people who see in a big way and immediately imagine they can do everything. There are petty officers, for example, who imagine themselves capable of winning all the battles of the world, and small people who think they surpass everybody in the world. On the other hand, I have known some people who had abilities but who spent their times thinking, "I am good for nothing." Generally the two extremes are found in the same person. But to find someone who knows exactly where he stands and exactly where he can go, is very rare. We have avoided speaking of vanity because we expect that you won't be filled with vanity as soon as you score a success.

Just imagine, there are plants which are vain! I am speaking of plants one grows for oneself. If one pays them compliments, by words or by feelings, if one admires them, well, they hold up their head—with vanity! It is the same with animals. I am going to tell you a short amusing story.

In Paris there is a garden called "The Garden of Plants": there are animals there also, as well as plants. They had just received a magnificent lion. It was of course in a cage. And it was furious. There was a door in the cage behind which it could hide. And it would hide itself just when the visitors came to see it! I saw that and one day I went up to the cage and began speaking to it (animals are very sensitive to spoken language, they really listen). I began speaking softly to my lion, I said to it, "Oh! how handsome you are, what a pity that you are hiding yourself like this, how much we would like to see you. . . . Well, it listened. Then, little by little, it looked at me askance, slowly stretched its neck to see me better; later it brought out its paw and, finally, put the tip of its nose against the bars as if saying, "At last, here's someone who understands me!"

"To be generous"

I shall not speak here of material generosity which naturally consists in giving others what one has. But even this virtue is not very widespread, for as soon as one becomes rich one thinks more often of keeping one's wealth than of giving it away. The more men possess, the less are they generous.

I want to speak of moral generosity. To feel happy, for example, when a comrade is successful. An act of courage, of unselfishness, a fine sacrifice have a beauty in them which gives you joy. It may be said that moral generosity consists in being able to recognise the true worth and superiority of others. (4-29,30)

Be Unselfish

Sweet Mother, ought we to do some other work besides studies?

Some other work? That depends upon you. It depends upon each one and on what one wants. If you want to do sadhana, it is obvious that you must have at least partially an occupation which is not selfish, that is, which is not done for oneself alone. Studies are all very well—very necessary, even quite indispensable, only it is a part of what I was speaking about just a while ago, that you must learn when you are young, for when you are grown-up it becomes much more difficult—but there is an age when you can have the foundation of indispensable studies and when, if you want to begin to do sadhana, you must do something which does not have an exclusively personal motive. One must do something a little unselfish, for if one is exclusively occupied with oneself, one gets shut up in a sort of carapace and is not open to the universal forces. A small unselfish movement, a small action done with no egoistic aim opens a door upon something other than one's own small, very tiny person.

One is usually shut up in a shell and becomes aware of other shells only when there is a shock or friction. But the consciousness of the circulating Force, of the interdependence of being—this is very rare thing. It is one of the indispensable stages of sadhana. (6-153)

Condition of the Earth

This is the condition of the earth, and it is not very bright. But for us one possibility remains—I have spoken about it to you several times already—even if, outside, things are deteriorating completely and the catastrophe cannot possibly be avoided, there remains for us, I mean those for whom the supramental life is not a vain dream, those who have faith in its reality and the aspiration to realise it—I don't necessarily mean those who have gathered here in Pondicherry, in the Ashram, but those who have a link between them the knowledge Sri Aurobindo has given and the will to live according to that knowledge—there remains for them the possibility of intensifying their aspiration, their will, their effort, to gather their energies together and shorten the time for the realisation. There remains for them the possibility of working this miracle—individually and to a small extent collectively—of conquering space, duration, the time needed for this realisation; of replacing time by intensity of effort and going fast enough and far enough in the realisation to liberate themselves from the consequences of the present condition of the world; of making such a concentration of force, strength, light, truth, that by this very realisation they can be above these consequences and secure against them, enjoy the protection bestowed by the Light and Truth, by Purity—the divine Purity through the inner transformation—and that the storm may pass over the world without being able to destroy this great hope of the near future; that the tempest may not sweep away this beginning of realisation. (9-169)

Notes to Chapter 5

[1] "If you look from one plane of consciousness, the individual will appear to you as if he were not only an instrument and recorder, but a creator. But look from another and higher plane of consciousness with a wider view of things and you will see that this is only an appearance. In

the workings of the universe whatever happens is the result of all that has happened before. How do you propose to separate one being from the integral play of the manifestation or one movement from the whole mass of movements? Where are you going to put the origin of a thing or its beginning?

6

OBSTACLES

Eastern thought and Integral Yoga have little place for the concepts of guilt and sin that are so prevalent to us in the West. The East places more emphasis on the concept of Ignorance—ignorance of our own essential self, our oneness of being. To return to that Oneness is the quest. The obstacles are numerous.

Our quest for progress is obstructed by various resistances both from personal habits and self-contradictions within our own nature and from our love of limitations. After all, these limitations have defined our sense of being and have made us to feel separate from everyone else. In the practice of Integral Yoga, we can transcend these limitations to experience the unity of Beingness and yet simultaneously maintain our sense of unique personality. This concept is unique and essential to Integral Yoga for this transformed personality must continue to be an effective instrument on this planet.

Obstacles
Limitations Imposed by Our Environment

"What is the nature of these influences from outside? Could you give us an explanation of their working?"

Naturally these influences are of very diverse kinds. They may be studied from a psychological point of view or from an almost mechanical standpoint, the one usually translating the other, that is, the mechanical phenomenon occurs as a sort of result of the psychological one.

In very few people, and even in the very best at very rare moments in life, does the will of the being express that deep inner, higher truth.

(*After a silence Mother continues:*) The individual consciousness extends far beyond the body; we have seen that even the subtle physical which is yet material compared with the vital being and in certain conditions almost visible, extends at times considerably beyond the visible limits of the physical body. This subtle physical is constituted of active vibrations which enter into contact or mingle with the vibrations of the subtle physical of others, and this reciprocal contact gives rise to influences—naturally the most powerful vibrations get the better of the others. For example, as I have already told you several times, if you have a thought, this thought clothes itself in subtle vibrations and becomes an entity which travels and moves about in the earth-atmosphere in order to realise itself as best it can, and because it is one among millions, naturally there is a multiple and involved interaction as a result of which things don't take place in such a simple and schematic fashion.

What you call yourself, the individual being enclosed within the limits of your present consciousness, is constantly penetrated by vibrations of this kind, coming from outside and very often presenting themselves in the form of suggestions, in the sense that, apart from a few exceptions, the action takes place first in the mental field, then becomes vital, then physical. I want to make it clear that it is not a question of the pure mind here, but of the physical mind; for in the physical consciousness itself there is a mental activity, a vital activity and a purely material activity, and all that takes place in your physical consciousness, in your body consciousness and bodily activity, penetrates first in the form of vibrations of a mental nature, and so in the form of suggestions. Most of the time these suggestions enter you without your being in the least conscious of them; they go in, awaken some sort of response in you, then spring up in your consciousness as though they were your own thought, your own will, your own impulse; but it is only because you are unconscious of the process of their penetration.

These suggestions are very numerous, manifold, varied, with natures which are very, very different from each other, but they may be classified into three principal orders. First—and they are hardly perceptible to the ordinary consciousness; they become perceptible only to those who have already reflected much, observed much, deeply studied their own being—they are what could be called collective suggestions.

When a being is born upon earth, he is invevitably born in a certain country and a certain environment. Due to his physical parents he is born in a set of social, cultural, national, sometimes religious circumstances, a set of habits of thinking, of understanding, of feeling, conceiving, all sorts of constructions which are at first mental, then become vital habits and finally material modes of being. To put things more clearly, you are born in a certain society or religion, in a particular country, and this society has a collective conception of its own and this nation has a collective conception of its own, this religion has a collective "construction" of its own which is usually very fixed. You are born into it. Naturally, when you are very young, you are altogether unaware of it, but it acts on your formation—that formation, that slow formation through hours and hours, through days and days, experiences added to experiences, which gradually builds up a consciousness. You are underneath it as beneath a bell-glass. It is a kind of construction which covers and in a way protects you, but in other ways limits you considerably. All this you absorb without even being aware of it and this forms the subconscious basis of your own construction. This subconscious basis will act on you throughout your life, if you do not take care to free yourself from it. And to free yourself from it, you must first of all become aware of it; and the first step is the most difficult, for this formation was so subtle, it was made when you were not yet a conscious being, when you had just fallen altogether dazed from another world into this one (*laugh-*

ing) and it all happened without your participating in the least in it. Therefore, it does not even occur to you that there could be something to know there, and still less something you must get rid of. And it is quite remarkable that when for some reason or other you do become aware of the hold of this collective suggestion, you realise at the same time that a very assiduous and prolonged labour is necessary in order to get rid of it. But the problem does not end there.

You live surrounded by people. These people themselves have desires, stray wishes, impulses which are expressed through them and have all kinds of causes, but take in their consciousness an individual form. For example, to put it in very practical terms: you have a father, a mother, brothers, sisters, friends, comrades; each one has his own way of feeling, willing, and all those with whom you are in relation expect something from you, even as you expect something from them. That something they do not always express to you, but it is more or less conscious in their being, and it makes formations. These formations, according to each one's capacity of thought and the strengths of his vitality, are more or less powerful, but they have their own little strength which is usually much the same as yours; and so what those around you want, desire, hope or expect from you enters in this way in the form of suggestions very rarely expressed, but which you absorb without resistance and which suddenly awaken within you a similar desire, a similar will, a similar impulse. . . . This happens from morning to night, and again from night to morning, for these things don't stop while you are sleeping, but on the contrary are very often intensified because your consciousness is no longer awake, watching and protecting you to some extent.

And this is quite common, so common that it is quite natural and so natural that you need special circumstances and most unusual occasions to become aware of it. Naturally, it goes without saying that your own responses, your own impulses, your own wishes have a similar influence on others, and that all this becomes a marvellous mixture in which might is always right!

If that were the end of the problem, one could yet come out of the mess; but there is a complication. This terrestrial world, this human world is constantly invaded by the forces of the neighbouring world, that is, of the vital world, the subtler region beyond the fourfold earth- atmosphere;[1] and this vital world which is not under the influence of the psychic forces or the psychic consciousness is essentially a world of ill-will, of disorder, disequilibrium, indeed of all the most anti-divine things one could imagine. This vital world is constantly penetrating the physical world, and being much more subtle than the physical it is very often quite imperceptible except to a few rare individuals. There are entities, beings, wills, various kinds of individualities in that world, who have all kinds of intentions and make use of every opportunity either to amuse themselves if they are small beings or to do harm and create disorder if they are beings with a greater capacity. And the latter have a very considerable power of penetration and suggestion, and wherever there is the least opening, the least affinity, they rush in, for it is a game which delights them.

Besides, they are very thirsty or hungry for certain human vital vibrations which for them are a rare dish they love to feed upon; and so their game lies in exciting pernicious movements in man so that man may emanate these forces and they be able to feed on them just as they please. All movements of anger, violence, passion, desire, all these things which make you abruptly throw off certain energies from yourself, project them from yourself, are exactly what these entities of the vital world like best, for, as I said, they enjoy them like a sumptuous dish. Now, their tactics are simple: they send you a little suggestion, a little impulse, a small vibration which enters deep into you and through contagion or sympathy awakens in you the vibration necessary to make you throw off the force they want to absorb.

There it is a little easier to recognise the influence, for, if you are the least bit attentive, you become aware of something that has suddenly awakened within you. For example, those who are in the habit of losing their temper, if they have attempted ever so little to control their anger, they will find something coming from outside or rising from below which actually takes hold of their consciousness and arouses anger in them. I don't mean that everybody is capable of this discernment; I am speaking of those who have tried to understand their being and control it. These adverse suggestions are easier to distinguish than, for instance, your response to the will or desire of a being who is of the same nature as yourself, another human being, who consequently acts on you without this giving you a clear impression of something coming from outside: the vibrations are too alike, too similar in their nature, and you have to be much more attentive and have a much sharper discernment to realise that these movements which seem to come out from you are not really yours but come from outside. But with the adverse forces, if you are in the least sincere and observe yourself attentively, you become aware that it is something in the being which is responding to an influence, an impulse, a suggestion, even something at times very concrete, which enters and produces similar vibrations in the being.

There, now. That is the problem.

The remedy? . . . It is always the same: goodwill, sincerity, insight, patience—oh! an untiring patience and a perseverance which assures you that what you have not succeeded in doing today, you will succeed in doing another time, and makes you go on trying until you do succeed.

And this brings us back to Sri Aurobindo's sentence: if this control seems to you quite impossible today, well, that means that not only will it be possible, but that it will be realised later. (8-389,390,391,392,393,394)

Individual's Love of His/Her Own Limitations

Your movements become true, but you do not possess all the manifold riches of the Divine's activity. Still, within your sphere, you are able to see correctly and according to the truth of things—which is certainly more than what is called in yogic parlance knowledge by identity. For, the kind of identification taught by many disciplines extends your limits of perception without piercing to the innermost heart of an object: it sees from within it, as it were, but only its phenomenal aspect. For example, if you identify yourself with a tree, you become aware in the way in which a tree is aware of itself, yet you do not come to know everything about a tree for the simple reason that it is itself not possessed of such knowledge. You do share the tree's inner feeling, but you certainly do not understand the truth it stands for, any more than by being conscious of your own natural self you possess at once the divine reality which you secretly are. Whereas if you are one with the divine consciousness, you know—over and above how the tree feels—what the truth behind it is, in short, you know everything, because the divine consciousness knows everything.

Indeed, there are many means of attaining this unity. It may be done through aspiration, or surrender, or some other method. Each followed with persistence and sincerity leads to it. Aspiration is the dynamic push of your whole nature behind the resolution to reach the Divine. Surrender, on the other hand, may be defined as the giving up of the limits of your ego. To surrender to the Divine is to renounce your narrow limits and let yourself be invaded by it and made a centre for its play. But you must bear in mind that the universal consciousness so beloved of Yogis is not the Divine: you can break your limits horizontally if you like, but you will be quite mistaken if you take the sense of wideness and cosmic multiplicity to be the Divine. The universal movement is after all a mixture of falsehood and truth, so that to stop there is to be imperfect; for, you may very well share the cosmic consciousness without ever attaining the transcendent Truth. On the other hand, to go to the Divine is also to attain the universal realisation and yet remain free of falsehood.

The real bar to self-surrender, whether to the Universal or to the Transcendent, is the individual's love of his own limitations. It is a natural love, since in the very formation of the individual being there is a tendency to concentrate on limits. Without that, there would be no sense of separateness—all would be mixed, as happens quite often in the mental and vital movements of consciousness. It is the body especially which preserves separative individuality by not being so fluid. But once this separateness is established, there creeps in the fear of losing it—a healthy instinct in many respects, but misapplied with regard to the Divine. For, in the Divine you do not really lose your individuality: you only give up your egoism and become the true individual, the divine personality which is not temporary like the construction of the physical consciousness which is usually taken for your *self*. One touch of the divine consciousness and you see immediately that there is no loss in it. On the contrary, you acquire a true individual permanence which can survive a hundred deaths of the body, and all the vicissitudes of the vital-mental evolution. Without this transfiguring touch, you always go about in fear; with it, you gradually develop the power to make even your physical being plastic without losing its individuality. Even now, it is not entirely rigid, it is able to feel the conscious movements of others by a sort of sympathy which translates itself into nervous reactions to their joys and sufferings: it is also able to express your inner movements—it is well known that the face is an index and mirror to the mind. But only the divine consciousness can make the body responsive enough to reflect all the movements of the supramental immortality and be an expression of the true soul and, by being divinised, reach the acme of a supreme individuality which can even physically rise superior to the necessity of death and dissolution.

In conclusion, I should like to draw your attention to one point, for it very frequently obstructs true union. It is a great error to suppose that the Divine Will is always acting openly in the world. All that happens is not, in fact, divine: the Supreme Will is distorted in the manifestation owing to the combination of lower forces which translate it. They are the medium which falsifies its impetus and gives it an undivine result. If all that happened were indeed the flawless translation of it, how could you account for the distortions of the world? . . . Not that the Divine Will could not have caused the cosmic Ignorance. It is omnipotent and all possibilities are inherent in it: it can work out anything of which it sees the secret necessity in its original vision. And the first cause of the world is, of course, the Divine, though we must take care not to adjudge this fact mentally according to our petty ethical values. But once the conditions of the cosmos were laid down and the involution into nescience accepted as the basis of a progressive manifestation of the Divine out of all that seemed its very opposite, there took place a sort of division between the Higher and the Lower. The history of the world became a battle between the True and the False, in which the details are not all direct representations of the Divine's progressive action but rather distortions of it owing to the mass of resistance offered by the inferior Nature. If there were no such resistance, there would be nothing whatever to conquer in the world, for the world would be harmonious, a constant passage from one perfection to another instead of the conflict which it is—a game of hazards and various possibilities in which the Divine faces real opposition, real difficulty and often real temporary defeat on the way to the final victory. It is just this reality of the whole play that makes it no mere jest. The Divine Will actually suffers distortion the moment it touches the hostile forces in the Ignorance. Hence we must never slacken our efforts to change the world and bring about a different order. We must be vigilant to co-operate with the Divine and not placidly think that whatever happens is always the best. All depends upon the personal attitude. If, in the presence of circumstances that are on the point of occurring, you take the highest possible attitude—that is to say, if you put your consciousness in contact with the highest consciousness within your reach—you can be absolutely certain that in such a case what happens is the best that can happen to you. But as soon as you fall from this consciousness and come down into a lower state, then it is evident that what happens cannot be the best, since you are not in your best consciousness. As Sri Aurobindo once said, "What happened had to happen, but it could have been much better." Because the person to whom it happened was not in his highest consciousness, there was no other consequence possible; but if he had brought about a descent of the Divine,then, even if the situation in general had been inevitable, it would have turned out in a different way. What makes all the difference is how you receive the impulsion of the Divine Will.

You must rise very high before you can meet this Will in its plenary splendour of authenticity; not before you open your lower nature to it can it begin to manifest in terms of the Truth. You must, therefore, refrain from applying the merely Nietzschean standard of temporary success in order to differentiate the Divine from the undivine. For, life is a battlefield in which the Divine succeeds in detail only when the lower nature is receptive to its impulsions instead of siding with the hostile forces. And even then the test is not so much external as internal: a divine movement cannot be measured by apparent signs—it is a certain kind of vibration that indicates its presence— external tests are of no avail, since even what is in appearance a failure may be in fact a divine achievement. . . . What you have to do is to give yourself up to the Grace of the Divine; for, it is under the form of Grace, of Love, that it has consented to uplift the universe after the first involution was established. With the Divine Love is the supreme power of Transformation. It has this power because it is for the sake of Transformation that it has given itself to the world and manifested everywhere. Not only has it infused itself into man, but also into all the atoms of the most obscure Matter in order to bring the world back to the original Truth. It is this descent that is called the supreme sacrifice in the Indian scriptures. But it is a sacrifice only from the human point of view; the human mind thinks that if it had to do such a thing it would be a tremendous sacrifice. But the Divine cannot really be diminished, its infinite essence can never become less, no matter what "sacrifices" are made. . . . The moment you open to the Divine Love, you also receive its power of Transformation. But it is not in terms of quantity that you can measure it; what is essential is the true contact; for, you will find that the true contact with it is sufficient to fill at once the whole of your being. (3-168,169,170,171,172)

Overcoming An Ignorance

When you make a mistake because you don't know that it is a mistake, through ignorance, it is obvious that when you learn that it is a mistake, when the ignorance has gone and you have goodwill, you don't make the mistake any more, and so you come out of the condition in which you could make it. But if you know it is a mistake and make it, this means that there is something perverse in you which has deliberately chosen to be on the side of confusion or bad will or even the anti-divine forces.

And it is quite obvious that if one chooses to be on the side of the anti-divine forces or is so weak and inconsistent that one can't resist the temptation to be on their side, it is infinitely more serious from the psychological point of view. This means that somewhere something has been corrupted: either an adverse force is already established in you or else you have an innate sympathy for these forces. And it is much more difficult to correct that than to correct an ignorance.

Correcting an ignorance is like eliminating darkness: you light a lamp, the darkness disappears. But to make a mistake once again when you know it is a mistake, is as if someone lighted a lamp and you deliberately put it out. . . . That corresponds exactly to bringing the darkness back deliberately. For the argument of weakness does not hold. The divine Grace is *always* there to help those who have decided to correct themselves, and they cannot say, "I am too weak to correct myself." They can say that they still haven't taken the resolution to correct themselves, that somewhere in the being there is something that has *not decided* to do it, and that is what is serious.

The argument of weakness is an excuse. The Grace is there to give the supreme strength to whoever takes the resolution.

That means an insincerity, it does not mean a weakness. And insincerity is always an open door for the adversary. That means there is some secret sympathy with what is perverse. And that is what is serious.

In the case of ignorance which is to be enlightened, it is enough, as I said, to light the lamp. In the case of conscious relapse, what is necessary is a cauterisation. (9-306,307)

Habits-Formation

What is the difference between the "old habits" and the "old formations" Sri Aurobindo speaks about?

It is almost the same thing. Your body, for instance, has certain reactions to cold, heat, hunger, and you are in the habit of having these reactions, and this habit has made a kind of formation in your physical nature, that is, a crease, a fixed crease of the body, and that's how it is. Formations are the result of habits. Similarly, there are "formations" of character; for instance, if you are in the habit of getting angry when things do not please you, the habit makes a sort of inner crease in your nature, and every time a thing doesn't please you, automatically, without any control, you will get angry. This is what is called a "formation", they are habits which have become like a part of your character. (4-345)

Limitations of Morality

Morality is something altogether artificial and arbitrary, and in most cases, among the best, it checks the true spiritual effort by a sort of moral satisfaction that one is on the right path and a true gentleman, that one does one's duty, fulfils all the moral requirements of life. Then one is so self-satisfied that one no longer moves or makes any progress.

It is very difficult for a virtuous man to enter the path of God; this has been said very often, but it is altogether true, for he is *most* self-satisfied, he thinks he has realised what he ought to have realised, he no longer has either the aspiration or even that elementary humility which makes one want to progresss. You see, one who is known here as a sattwic man[2] is usually very comfortably settled in his own virtue and never thinks of coming out of it. So, that puts you a million leagues away from the divine realisation.

What really helps, until one has found the inner light, is to make for oneself a certain number of rules which naturally should not be too rigid and fixed, but yet should be precise enough to prevent one from going completely out of the right path or making irreparable mistakes—mistakes the consequences of which one suffers all one's life.

To do that, it is good to set up a certain number of principles in oneself, which, however, should be for each one, in conformity with his own nature. If you adopt a social, collective rule, you immediately make yourself a slave to this social rule, and that prevents you almost radically from making any effort for transformation. (8-143)

Contradictions in our Make-Up Hold the Key to Victory

Difficulties in Yoga

The nature of your difficulty indicates the nature of the victory you will gain, the victory you will exemplify in Yoga. Thus, if there is persistent selfishness, it points to a realisation of universality as your most prominent achievement in the future. And, when selfishness is there, you have also the power to reverse this very difficulty into its opposite, a victory of utter wideness.

When you have something to realise, you will have in you just the characteristics which is the contradiction of that something. Face to face with the defect, the difficulty, you say, "Oh, I am like that! How awful it is!" But you ought to see the truth of the situation. Say to yourself, "My difficulty shows me clearly what I have ultimately to represent. To reach the absolute negation of it, the quality at the other pole—this is my mission."

Even in ordinary life, we have sometimes the experience of contraries. He who is very timid and has no courage in front of circumstances proves capable of bearing the most!

To one who has the aspiration for the Divine, the difficulty which is always before him is the door by which he will attain God in his own individual manner: it is his particular path towards the Divine Realisation.

There is also the fact that if somebody has a hundred difficulties it means he will have a tremendous realisation—provided, of course, there are in him patience and endurance and he keeps the aspiring flame of Agni burning against those defects.

And remember: the Grace of the Divine is generally proportioned to your difficulties. (3-143)

Adverse Forces Test Us Through Their Opposition and Resistance

Sometimes when an adverse force attacks us and we come out successful, why are we attacked once again by the same force?

Because something was left inside. We have said that the force can attack only when there is something which responds in the nature—however slight it may be. There is a kind of affinity, something corresponding, there is a disorder or an imperfection which attracts the adverse force by responding to it. So, if the attack comes, you must keep perfectly quiet and send it back, but it does not necessarily follow that you have got rid of that small part in you which allows the attack to come.

You have something in you which attracts this force; take, for example (it is one of the most frequent things), the force of depression, that kind of attack of a wave of depression that falls upon you: you lose confidence, you lose hope, you have the feeling you will never be able to do anything, you are cast down. It means there is in your vital being something which is naturally egoistic, surely a little vain, which needs encouragement to remain in a good state. So it is like a little signal for those forces which intimates to them: "You can come, the door is open." But there is another part in the being that was watching when these forces arrived; instead of allowing them to enter, the part which sees clearly, which knows, which has power, which resists, says: "No, I do not want that, it is not true, I do not want it", and sends them back. But you have not necessarily been cured of the little thing within you which permitted them to come. You must go very deep within, work within you persistently to be able to efface all possibility of calling. And so long as you have not completely effaced it, the attack will recur almost unexpectedly. You push it back—it is like a ball you throw against the wall, back it returns; you push it back once again and again it returns—until the moment there is no longer anything to attract it. Then it does not return again.

Therefore, the most important thing to do when you are attacked by an adverse force, is to say to yourself: "Yes, the force comes from outside and the attack is there, but there must certainly be a correspondence in my nature, otherwise it could not have attacked me. Well, I am going to look and find within me what allows this force to come and I am going to sent it back or transform it or put the light of consciousness upon it so that it may be converted, or drive it away so that it remains no longer within me. . . . " There is a way, isn't there? When the force comes, the adverse force, when it attacks, the part which corresponds rushes out to meet it, it goes forward. A kind of meeting takes place. If at that time, instead of being altogether overwhelmed or taken by surprise and off your guard, you observe very closely what it was within you that vibrated (it makes the sound tat, tat, tat: another thing has entered), then you can catch it. At that moment, you catch it and say to it: "Get out with your friends, I don't want you any longer!" You send away the two together, the part that attracted and the thing it attracted; they are sent away and you are absolutely clear. (5-94,95,96)

Resistance

> *You have said that on the material plane "receptivity is mixed with a large amount of resistance."*[3] *What is this resistance?*

Don't you have resistances in your body, don't you? When you want to do an exercise, can you do with your body whatever you want? And when you try to be in good health, does your body always obey? And when you want to learn your lesson, does your brain follow it without difficulty? . . . That is the resistance, it is all that refuses to progress.

And I believe that unfortunately the amount of resistance is much greater than the amount of receptivity. One must work very hard to become receptive.

One does not know—it is perhaps something you will know one day, perhaps one will be able to make you understand it—you cannot imagine the immense flood of force at your disposal! And generally you do not feel it even. When you feel it, something in you shrinks because it is too much and produces a kind of instinctive fear in your cells; and when you receive it, more than three quarters of it you throw away like an overfilled vessel! It gushes out, spills over, because you are not able to hold it. I have met a very large number of people who complained that they were receiving nothing, that is to say, they said they did not have the forces they needed. It was because they were absolutely incapable of receiving them, and there was a hundred thousand times more force than what they could receive. It is like that. You are all in a sea of tremendous vibrations, and you are not at all aware of it because you are not receptive. And there is such a resistance in you that if something succeeds in entering, three quarters of what enters is thrown out violently because you are not able to contain it. . . . I do not speak of this usually, but since we are talking about the subject, I am telling you. And perhaps one day I shall give you examples of it. It is something unbelievable. For example, just take the consciousness of the Forces, like the force of love, the force of understanding or the force of creation (for everything, it is the same: the force of protection, the force of growth, all that, and the power for progress, for everything); take Consciousness, simply this Consciousness which surrounds everything, enters into everything, which is everywhere, which is in everything. . . . Well, it is almost felt as a violence which seeks to impose itself upon the being that is unable to receive or bear it. And I am speaking of the very best; but in everyone there is a part more or less big, more or less important which does not yet have the goodwill, which is just on the border-line of bad will and does not want at any cost and rejects what is there. But if one were open and simply breathed in—nothing more, if one did that only—one would breathe in the Consciousness, the Light, the Understanding, the Force, the Love and all the rest. And all that is wasted upon Earth because the Earth is not ready to take it. (5-270,271)

Talking

Very often I have told you that every word spoken uselessly is dangerous chatter. (9-143)

What should be done to refrain from talking?

Think! You have only to reflect a little more. If only you make it a habit to think before speaking, that saves you at least half of what you say. To think before speaking and to say only what seems absolutely indispensable to you—then you very quickly become aware that very few words are indispensable, except from the practical point of view, in work, when one is working with somebody and is obliged to use words: "Do this", "Give me that", or "Like this", or "Like that". And even so, this can be reduced to a minimum. (6-223)

Overcoming Reaction to Criticism

How can one become indifferent to criticism?

By climbing somewhere up on the ladder—in one's own consciousness—looking at things a little more vastly, a little more generally. For example, if at a particlar moment there is something which holds you, grips you like that, holds you tight, close pressed, and you absolutely want it to happen, and you are fighting against a terrible obstacle, you see something which is preventing it from happening; if simply just at that moment you begin to feel, to realise the myriads and myriads of years there were before this present moment, and the myriads and myriads of years there will be after this present moment, and what importance this little event has in relation to all that—there is no need to enter a spiritual consciousness or anything else, simply enter into relation with space and time, with all that is before, all that is after and all that is happening at the same time—if one is not an idiot, immediately he tells himself, "Oh, well, I am attaching importance to something which doesn't have any." Necessarily so, you see. It loses all its importance, immediately.

If you can visualise, you know, simply the immensity of the creation—I am not now speaking of rising to spiritual heights—simply the immensity of the creation in time and space, and this little event on which you are concentrated with an importance . . . as though it were something of some importance . . . immediately it does this (*gesture*) and it dissolves, if you do it sincerely. If, naturally, there is one part of yourself which tells you, "Ah, but for me it has an importance", then, there, you have only to leave that part behind and keep your consciousness as it is. But if sincerely you want to see the true value of things, it is very easy.

There are other methods, you know. There is a Chinese sage who advises you to lie down upon events as one floats on one's back upon the sea, imagining the immensity of the ocean and that you let yourself go floating upon this . . . upon the waves, you see, like something contemplating the skies and letting itself be carried away. In Chinese they call this *Wu Wei*. When you can do this all your troubles are gone. I knew an Irishman who used to lie flat on his back and look outside, as much as possible on an evening when stars were in the sky, he looked, contemplated the sky and imagined that he was floating in that immensity of countless luminous points.

And immediately all troubles are calmed.

There are many ways. But sincerely, you have only to . . . have the sense of relativity between your little person and the importance you give to the things which concern you, and the universal immensity; this is enough. Naturally there is another way, it is to free oneself from the earth consciousness and rise into a higher consciousness where these terrestrial things take their true place—which is quite small, you see. (7-396,397)

Silence Is Golden

In fact, for the physical being—note that I say the physical being—to be fully developed, it must have twelve senses. It is one of these senses which gives you the kind of perception I was speaking of. You cannot say that it is taste, smell, hearing, etc., but it is something which gives you a very precise impression of the difference of quality. And it is very precise, as distinct as seeing black and white, it is truly a sense perception.

Generally, when you want to study occultism, the first thing that the Master does is never to speak to you about it, never to explain it to you, precisely because of this ridiculous phenomenon of the mind which begins to "think" about it and brings you "experiences" which have no value: they are mental formations which make a plaything of you, that is all. They have no reality.

You must distrust the mind altogether when you want to enter the world of experiences. It is enough for the mind to be just slightly roused for it to say, "Ah, what is going on?" . . . Then it may be that things do happen but it is no longer *the* thing, it is a fabrication.

First condition, know how to keep silent. And not only keep your tongue quiet, but silence your mind, keep the head silent. If you wish to have a true, sincere experience upon which you can build, you must know how to be silent, otherwise you have nothing but what you fabricate yourself, which is equivalent to zero. All that one can say is, "Heavens, what a fashioner my mind is!" (4-230,231)

Weak Nervous System

Some people have a well-developed body but in spite of that they are very nervous. Then . . . ?

Usually it is . . . Perhaps they have a very weak vital build: their nerves may be weak, they may have a weak nervous system; perhaps it is that, perhaps it is an irregularity from birth. But it could also be a mental weakness, because while it is true that a healthy body gives strong nerves, it is still more important to have healthy thoughts in order to have solid nerves. If your thought is not healthy, if your feelings and thoughts are bad so to speak, your nerves become very bad, still worse. For instance, those who entertain all kinds of unhealthy fancies, those who like unhealthy reading, unhealthy conversations—there are many of this kind, there is a large number of them—well, they may lose all control over their nerves, they may become extremely nervous and yet have a body that's in a fine condition and very healthy. Unhealthy conversations and reading—I can tell you that there's nothing worse than that, and when you do sadhana truly, when you are really trying to progress, you notice that when you say useless words, no matter how few they are, immediately there is a terrible uneasiness which gets hold of you; you feel as though all the nerves of the head were being pulled and there is also something churning here (*gesture*) which hurts you, and you feel a great emptiness within and have heartburn, as though you had eaten something very bad—all this only because of some uselessly spoken words. Besides, it is a sure indication: as soon as the uneasiness begins, one knows one must stop: "Now it is finished." Only, most people are so unconscious that they don't even notice it, and with their warped will they compel their system to do what it should not. So, the system is more or less docile, obeys and continues to deteriorate slowly, in this way, without even showing visible reactions. (6-76)

Telling Lies and Being Judgmental

Instead of that, you search: "What can be the motive of one who tells lies? . . . " and you push—you push and all of a sudden you discover in a little corner something which wants to justify itself, thrust itself forward or assert its own way of seeing (no matter what, there are a number of reasons), show itself a little different from what it is so that people may have a good opinion of you and think you someone very remarkable. . . . It was that which spoke in you—not your active consciousness, but what was there and pushed the consciousness from behind. When you were not quite on your guard, it made use of your mouth, your tongue, and then there you were! the lie came out. I am giving you this example—there are a million others. And it is extremely interesting. And to the extent one discovers this within oneself and says sincerely, "It must change", one finds that one acquires a sort of inner clear-sightedness, one gradually becomes aware of what goes on in others, and instead of flying into a temper when they are not quite what one would like them to be, one begins to understand how things happen, how it is that one is "like this", how reactions are produced. . . . Then, with the indulgence of knowledge, one smiles. One no longer judges severely, one offers the difficulty in oneself or in others, whatever may be its centre of manifestation, to the divine Consciousness, asking for its transformation. (4-338)

Cowardice

Sweet Mother, when we are faced with a difficulty, does this mean that the Divine is trying to make us conscious of the defects of our nature?

If you face it, yes. That is, as soon as you are in front of a difficulty, if instead of giving way like a coward you begin trying to conquer it, then you may be sure that the Divine is behind you. But if you are cowardly, the Divine will not be there. That is, your cowardice cuts you off from the Divine. But if you resist and want to conquer, you may be sure that the Divine will be there to help you. There's not the shadow of a doubt about it.

But I want to know—if the difficulty comes—whether the Divine is trying to make us conscious that we have defects?

Whether he deliberately puts difficulties in your path? No. (6-461)

Mantra

And then, you may also take another attitude. When you are playing and suddenly become aware that something is going wrong—you are making mistakes, are inattentive, sometimes opposing currents come across what you are doing—if you develop the habit, automatically at this moment, of calling as by a mantra, of repeating a word, that has an extraordinary effect. You choose your mantra; or rather, one day it comes to you spontaneously in a moment of difficulty. At a time when things are very difficult, when you have a sort of anguish, anxiety, when you don't know what is going to happen, suddenly this springs up in you, the word springs up in you. For each one it may be different. But if you mark this and each time you face a difficulty you repeat it, it becomes irresistible. For instance, if you feel you are about to fall ill, if you feel you are doing badly what you are doing, if you feel something evil is going to attack you, then. . . . But it must be a spontaneity in the being, it must spring up from you without your needing to think about it: you choose your mantra because it is a spontaneous expression of your aspiration; it may be one word, two or three words, a sentence, that depends on each one, but it must be a sound which awakens in you a certain condition. Then, when you have that, I assure you that you can pass through everything without difficulty. Even in the face of a real, veritable danger, an attack, for instance, by someone who wants to kill you, if, without getting excited, without being perturbed, you quietly repeat your mantra, one can do nothing to you. Naturally, you must truly be master of yourself; one part of the being must not be trembling there like a leaf; no, you must do it entirely, sincerely, then it is all-powerful. The best is when the word comes to you spontaneously: you call in a moment of great difficulty (mental, vital, physical, emotional, whatever it may be) and suddenly that springs up in you, two or three words, like magical words. You must remember these and form the habit of repeating them in moments when difficulties come. If you form the habit, one day it will come to you spontaneously: when the difficulty comes, at the same time the mantra will come. Then you will see that the results are wonderful. But it must not be an artificial thing or something you arbitrarily decide: "I shall use those words"; nor should somebody else tell you, "Oh! you know, this is very good"—it is perhaps very good for him but not for everyone. (4-389,390)

Raising Energy to the Chakras

Generally, it is said that there are five. But the true number is seven or even twelve. Anyway, these centres are centres of accumulation of energy, energies which control certain activities. Thus, there is an accumulation of energy at the sex-centre, a great accumulation of energy, and those who have control over these energies succeed in mastering them and raising them up, and they place them here (*Mother points to the centre of the chest*). And here is the centre of the energies of progress. This is what is called the seat of *Agni* [Divine Will], but it is the energies of progress, the will to progress, that are here. So the energies concentrated in the sex-centre are pulled upwards and placed here. And they increase considerably, so that the sex-centre becomes absolutely calm, peaceful, immobile.

The ordinary practice for controlling these energies is to

manage to "uncoil" the Kundalini [Energy] which is coiled up at the base of the spine and raise the energies through the spinal column to the different centres, and awaken the centres, open them, wake them up and set them in motion one after another right up to the top of the head, and then, go out from up there. And when one has succeeded in doing this (this is the first practice), when one has uncoiled the Kundalini, next to master it, guide and develop it, to guide it to all the centres, awaken all these centres. Once that has been done, one is master of the functioning. Once one is master of the functioning, instead of leaving the energies in places where they are not wanted, one pulls them up and puts them in places where they are useful, and uses them in this way for progress, for transformation.

All this is the result of enlightened, assiduous, very patient practice; this is not done *just like that*, while thinking of other things or playing about. These are disciplines. Naturally, once one is master of the working, it becomes very interesting. But this is not done in a flash without one's doing what is necessary. (6-77,78)

Pleasure Vs. Bliss

"*She has come*, bringing with her a splendour of power and love, an intensity of divine joy unknown to the earth so far.

The physical atmosphere was completely changed by it, saturated with new and marvellous possibilities. For, of all the aspects of the Mother, this is the one which has the greatest power for the transformation of the body. Indeed, the cells which are able to vibrate to the contact of divine joy, to receive and preserve it, are regenerated cells on the way to becoming immortal. But the vibrations of divine joy and those of pleasure cannot lodge together in the same vital and physical system. So one must have *totally* renounced experiencing all pleasure in order to be in a state to receive the Ananda [Bliss]. But very few are those who can renounce pleasure without, by the very fact, renouncing all participation in active life and plunging into a rigorous asceticism. And among those who know that it is in active life that the transformation must take place, some try to see pleasure as a more or less warped form of Ananda, and thus justify in themselves the quest for personal satisfaction, creating in themselves an almost insuperable obstacle to their own transformation." (6-291,292)

Success—The Last Test

You must not judge things from an outer success or a semblance of defeat. We may say—and generally this is what almost always happens—we could say that the Divine gives what one desires, and of all lessons this is the best! For, if your desire is inconscient, obscure, egoistic, you increase the unconsciousness, the darkness and egoism within yourself; that is to say, this takes you farther and farther away from the truth, from consciousness and happiness. It takes you far away from the Divine. And for the Divine, naturally, only one thing is true—the divine Consciousness, the divine Union. And each time you put material things in front, you become more and more materialistic and go father and farther away from full success.

But for the Truth that other success is a terrible defeat. . . . You have exchanged truth for falsehood!

To judge from appearances and apparent success is precisely an act of complete ignorance. Even for the most hardened man, for whom everything has apparently been successful, even for him there is always a counterpart. And this kind of hardening of the being which is produced, this veil which is formed, a thicker and thicker veil, between the outer consciousness and the inner truth, becomes, one day or another, altogether intolerable. It is usually paid for very dearly—outer success.

(*Mother's voice becomes extremely deep.*) One must be *very* great, *very* pure, have a *very* high and *very* disinterested spiritual consciousness in order to be successful without being affected by it. *Nothing is more difficult than being successful. This, indeed, is the true test of life!*

When you do not succeed, quite naturally you turn back on yourself and within yourself, and you seek within yourself the consolation for your outer failure. And to those who have a flame within them—if the Divine really wants to help them, if they are mature enough to be helped, if they are ready to follow the path—blows will come one after another, because this helps! It is the most powerful, the most direct, most effective help. If you succeed, be on your guard, ask yourself: "At what price, what cost have I bought success? I hope it is not a step towards . . . " (6-238,239)

Falsehood

The lords of Falsehood hold, at present, almost complete sway over poor humanity. Not only the lower life-energy, the lower vital being, but also the whole mind of man accepts them. Countless are the ways in which they are worshipped, for they are most subtle in their cunning and seek their ends in variously seductive disguises. The result is that men cling to their falsehood as if it were a treasure, cherishing it more than even the most beautiful things of life. Apprehensive of its safety, they take care to bury it deep down in themselves; but unless they take it out and surrender it to the Divine they will never find true happiness.

Indeed the very act of bringing it out and showing it to the Light would be in itself a momentous conversion and pave the way to the final victory. For the laying bare of each falsehood is in itself a victory—each acknowledgment of error is the demolition of one of the lords of Darkness. It may be an acknowledgment to oneself, provided it is absolutely honest and is no subtle regret apt to be forgotten the next moment and without the strength to make an unbreakable resolution not to repeat the mistake. Or it may be the acknowledgment to the Divine embodied in the Guru.

As a result of direct personal confession to the Guru, your resolution remains no longer your own, because, if you are sincere, the Divine's fiat goes forth in your favour. To give you an idea of what this means I shall relate an experience of mine when I first met Sri Aurobindo in Pondicherry. I was in deep concentration, seeing things in the Supermind, things that were to be but which were somehow not manifesting. I told Sri Aurobindo what I had seen and asked him if they would manifest. He simply said, "Yes." And immediately I saw that the Supramental had touched the earth and was beginning to be realised! This was the first time I had witnessed the power to make real what is true: it is the very same power that will bring about the realisation in you of the truth when you come in all sincerity, saying, "This falsehood I want to get rid of", and the answer which you get is "Yes." (3-141,142)

Notes to Chapter 6

[1] Consisting of the four principles: physical, vital, mental and psychic.

[2] According to the Indian terminology, a sattwic person is one who is moved by the principle of knowledge, equanimity and light, as opposed to a rajasic man who is moved by his desires and passions and a tamasic man who lives in inertia and obscurity.

[3] *Questions and Answers 1929* (16 June).